CRYSTALS

CRYSTALS

THE MODERN GUIDE TO
CRYSTAL HEALING

YULIA VAN DOREN | GOLDIROCKS

PHOTOGRAPHY BY ERIKA RAXWORTHY

Hardie Grant

QUADRILLE

Contents

Hello, magic maker.

Whether you're already a devoted member of the crystal-obsessed fan club (never far from at least a few beloved rocks), or are very newly crystal-curious (and wondering what all the fuss is about?) – welcome, I'm so glad you have found your way to this guidebook.

Crystals can fill your life with magic, their uniquely radiant and sparkling brand of magic. Born from the ancient rumblings and rattlings of our beautiful Earth, literally seeded by stardust from the dawn of time, crystals and minerals are magic-filled tools that are fantastically easy to add into your daily life. You don't need special knowledge or training to begin experiencing the power of crystals, and you certainly don't need to spend loads of money on expensive specimens. All you need to get started is a sense of wonder and open-minded curiosity towards the intricate, gorgeous and powerful creations that are minerals and crystals.

This guidebook is divided into two sections: **Crystal Magic 101** covers all the information and tools needed to jumpstart your crystalline adventures, and **The Crystals** is an in-depth guide to the 50 crystals I believe hold the most magic for our current time, intentionally chosen to be both accessible and affordable.

If this book has found its way to you, crystals hold magic for you to personally discover and experience. Trust your intuition, trust the power of magic, and keep your heart and spirit always open to the gifts that crystals will – magically, mysteriously, and most certainly – bring into your life.

may your life be full of magic!
Yulia / Goldirocks

You are made of stardust

'we are stardust, billion year old carbon, we are golden...'

— **Joni Mitchell,** *Woodstock*

Everything within and surrounding you at this very moment was born from stardust. Created by ancient cosmic events of unimaginable power and immensity, stardust infuses our entire universe and seeded life here on Planet Earth. And what is stardust made of? Stardust = minerals, minerals and more minerals.

As Madonna (almost) sang, we truly are 'living in a mineral world.' Beneath our feet lie unimaginable quantities and varieties of crystals and minerals within the earth. Above our heads sparkle the mineral clusters we call stars. Our buildings are crafted from minerals and crystals (steel = iron minerals, glass = melted crystals). Our cars, computers and phones work only because they contain a multitude of minerals and crystals that literally power them. Crystal technology isn't just some woo-woo, New Age concept, it is one of the essential building blocks of our modern technological age.

Crystals are enjoying a very bright moment in our collective consciousness. The glittering magic contained within Mother Earth's gems is beginning to resonate with a rapidly expanding tribe of people, who are exploring ways to experience crystals within daily life far beyond their obvious industrial uses. Although modern technology utilises the scientifically proven 'powers' of crystals, such as their piezoelectric capabilities (e.g. their ability to transform pressure into an electrical current), there is a community of crystal adventurers who are discovering new powers contained within crystals and minerals – ones which we believe modern science simply hasn't caught up with yet.

The mythology of crystals and minerals, as ancient and global as our human history, is experiencing a supercharged moment in our Modern New Age. And because working with crystals requires that each person tap into their intuition to find their own insights and healing, we are all writing this sparkling story together, continuing the legacy of crystals as a connected community of crystalline explorers. *What will you discover?*

Minerals and crystals and rocks, oh my...

krystallos: from the Ancient Greek, meaning 'crystallised light'

Our beautiful planet contains over 5000 identified minerals, with hundreds of new varieties being discovered each year – many crystal healers believe that new minerals surface as their particular energies are needed within the world. Although I like to be informal when talking about minerals/crystals/ rocks/gemstones/stones and interchange the terms, let's take a moment to get clear on their unique differences.

MINERALS are generally formed from only one chemical composition; more than one and they turn into *rocks* (see right). The definition of a mineral is: 1. Naturally occurring; 2. Solid; 3. Inorganic (i.e. not made from fossilised bits of ancient plants or animals); 4. Has an internal crystalline structure; however, not all minerals form crystals large enough to be visible to our human eyes. Which means that while all crystals are minerals, not all minerals are crystals. Examples of minerals that do not have a visible crystalline structure:

Malachite, Hematite, Carnelian

CRYSTALS generally refer to minerals with a visible crystallised form. This means that they show a faceted, symmetrical (e.g. cubic) or asymmetrical (e.g. rhombohedral), three-dimensional, geometric form. The astounding variety of crystals actually fits into just six categories, or 'crystal systems', each with its own unique geometric shape, making crystal identification much easier than it might seem at first glance. Examples of crystals:

Quartz, Pyrite, Fluorite

ROCKS are generally formed from grains of **multiple minerals** fused together into a solid mass. Rocks may contain organic material, which true minerals cannot (for example, Shungite is a rock made from ancient vegetation). Examples of rocks:

Jade, Obsidian, Lapis Lazuli

GEMSTONES are minerals or rocks **strong enough** to be cut and polished for jewellery. Only about 200 of the 5000+ minerals and rocks can be shaped into gemstones. Examples of gemstones:

Moonstone, Labradorite, Turquoise

STONES is a **non-technical** term, commonly used in the mineral world to refer to small specimens whose rough edges have been mechanically polished away, aka *tumbled stones* or *polished stones*.

POLISHED VS RAW

Perhaps similar to the belief that getting nutrients from real food is more potent than from a vitamin pill, many crystal lovers find something uniquely organic and powerful about a crystal left in its 'raw' form, as created by Mother Earth. There are, however, plenty of minerals who reveal hidden glamour only once polished: Rainbow Fluorite's beautiful layers are much more vibrant, as is the 'flash' within Labradorite and Moonstone, as examples. And polished crystals are also often easier to lay on the body for crystal healing, as well as handy for carrying around in all those little spots we love to tuck our rocks (bags, pockets, bras, etc). Just be aware that polishing can sometimes unnaturally 'freeze' a crystal's energy flow, so if a crystal doesn't feel alive to you in its polished form definitely try to get your hands on a raw specimen for comparison – the energy difference can be quite amazing!

A NOTE ABOUT MINING

Mining is a complicated subject with imperfect truths, but very important to address as crystal collectors. Simply put, many of the mineral specimens we treasure are by-products of industrial mining, preserved only because collectors ascribe value to keeping them in their whole form. The vast majority of mining is for industry, meaning that after minerals are mined they are processed for a huge variety of industrial uses: Iron-based minerals such as Hematite are melted for steel, Lithium-filled minerals like Lepidolite become batteries and pharmaceuticals, natural cosmetics use a variety of mineral pigments and clays, organic farmers fertilise with Aragonite and Sulphur... there truly isn't an area of modern life that doesn't utilise minerals in some form. Many of the crystals coming out of the ground today formed before our first ancestors walked this earth, and now that they've been extracted they need our careful care to ensure that they remain beautiful and whole. So treasure each of your rocks; there isn't another just like it in the entire universe!

HOW CRYSTALS WORK:
vibration + colour + talisman

Bringing sparkle and flash wherever they're placed, crystals top the list of nature's most stunning creations and have a long history of being treasured solely as organic home decor. However, their transformative powers go far deeper than just what meets the eye, and even when crystals are acquired purely for their good looks they can't help but infuse the spaces – and people – around them with a powerful combination of vibrational balancing, colour healing, and talismanic magic.

1. VIBRATION As the other-worldly inventor, Nikola Tesla, put it, *'If you want to find the secrets of the universe, think in terms of energy, frequency, and vibration.'* All of life dances with a magnetic pulse and vibration; from scientists we have learned that every atom in the universe is constantly in motion, and metaphysicians teach that every object is surrounded by its own vibrating sphere of energy, an 'aura'. Crystals are unique within nature as their atoms follow the most symmetrical pattern possible, creating what is called a 'crystal lattice'. *It is their perfect atomic symmetry that makes crystals such powerful holders and transmitters of energy and vibration.* Because being a human is a much 'messier' atomic arrangement, our atoms and auras are harmonised by interacting with the unique symmetry of crystals.

2. COLOUR The tradition of using colour for health and well-being has been practiced since ancient times, and *the vibrant colours of crystals are one of the most potent aspects of their healing power.* Science has proven that we are profoundly affected both physically and emotionally by the colours that surround us (think of how different you feel in a bright red vs pastel blue room), and on a metaphysical level, our chakra system is strongly energised and activated by specific colours. Crystals provide one of the easiest ways to add bright and organic pops of colour into our homes and workspaces, and will literally change your mood and energy with their uplifting rainbow hues.

3. TALISMAN Born from the Ancient Greek verb *telein*, meaning 'to initiate into mysteries', a talisman is traditionally defined as an object believed to hold magical or miraculous abilities, 'lucky charms' being the talismans us modern folk are probably most familiar with. When you choose to bring a crystal into your life for a specific intention or goal – Rose Quartz to find love, or Pyrite to gain confidence, for example – *your specific intention transforms a crystal into your own personalised, magic-filled talisman*. Crystals function as powerful accountability buddies. Their presence gives both your consciousness and subconsciousness helpful nudges whenever you're near, tirelessly reminding you of the person you wish to be, the energies you wish to hold, and the life you are ready to step into.

HOLISTIC HEALING Crystals regularly manifest their magic in what can be called a 'subtle', form, similar to other forms of holistic healing. To better understand the concept of subtle healing, imagine the difference between drinking a glass of wine and taking a vitamin. After just a few sips of wine you feel unmistakably altered; however the effect is fleeting and (fortunately!) not long term. In contrast, when you pop a vitamin you feel no different immediately, and you may even begin to wonder whether taking vitamins is effective. Take those vitamins daily, however, and one day you suddenly realise, 'Wow, I just feel so much better! That issue I've been having simply hasn't been bothering me, I haven't even thought about it lately!' **Almost without you noticing, things have subtly – yet very unmistakably – shifted within you.** Crystal healing often works via this type of subtle yet deep, long-term magic. However, many people have also experienced breathtakingly spontaneous and unexplainable moments of crystal healing so the best advice I can share with you regarding holistic healing is this: *Keep your mind and heart open to limitless possibility, and you will be amazed by what manifests around and within you.*

'And above all, watch with glittering eyes the whole world around
you because the greatest secrets are always hidden in the most
unlikely places. Those who don't believe in magic will never find it.'

— **Roald Dahl,** *The Minpins*

GET CRYSTALLISED:
crystal collecting

We are in the middle of a crystal heyday, with crystals sold everywhere from huge chain stores to hipster coffee shops (meaning that it's never been easier to feed a crystal addiction – you've been warned!).

CRYSTAL SHOPPING

Besides dedicated mineral stores, metaphysical (New Age) shops generally offer the best variety for in-person crystal shopping. Local mineral shows usually occur once a year and can be fun to visit, filled with friendly rockhounds and good deals: google your location + 'mineral show' to start your search. And of course, there's a huge variety of options for purchasing crystals online, from Instagram and Etsy, to eBay and boutique websites. I've added many amazing crystals to my personal collection via online shopping, so my best tips for remorse-free buying are 1. Buy only from sellers who accept returns; 2. Make sure you clearly understand the size (millimetres and centimetres are very different things!); 3. Order from a business whose vibe you resonate with, as the crystal has spent time in that vibrational environment.

CHOOSING YOUR CRYSTALS

If you've spent any time exploring the world of crystals I'm sure you've noticed that guidebooks often assign differing – sometimes even conflicting – metaphysical meanings and uses for the same crystal. Confused by which description to trust? Use that magical intuition of yours: if one description grabs you more than another, go with the one that resonates. **All crystals have expansive and multifaceted energies, and they all carry many gifts.** The meaning that resonates is the one holding magic specifically for you,

at this particular moment on your path. This means that buying personal crystals should also be simple and intuitive process: **very often, the first crystal to catch your eye – or the first you pick up – is the crystal which holds the most magic for you**. Don't overthink it. If you need help deciding, simply close your eyes, hold a crystal up to your heart or third eye chakra (between your eyebrows), and breathe. After a few breaths you should have a clear sense of whether that crystal is meant to come home with you. Another great way to intuitively grow your collection is to pay attention to which photographs and/or keywords jump out at you while flipping through this book; if your intuition is sparked, try to get your hands on a real-life specimen to see if it's an energetic match.

YOU DON'T NEED TO SPEND $$$

Some of my most treasured crystals are the most unassuming to look at. Dinged and scratched, chipped and cloudy, they aren't the crystals that win beauty prizes, and they weren't pricey, but they just felt *right* when

I saw them. **Powerful magic is often contained within humble exteriors**. Again, always trust your intuition when choosing your crystals, even if your eyes don't agree.

LOCAL STONES

Don't overlook the humble rocks that live beneath your feet, as they contain specific earth energies of the place in which you live, and are invaluable for grounding yourself in your current time and place (very important for mental peace and stability!). Stones from places meaningful to you – your birthplace, family home, beloved holiday spot, etc – are valuable holders of energies important to your personal story, and including them in your collection is highly recommended as long as the memories they spark for you are positive and grounding.

CRYSTAL CARE + FEEDING
cleansing + charging + programming

Cleansing and charging your crystals' energy – especially
when you first bring them home – is an important part of
being a crystal owner. Regularly spending even a bit of time
giving them love and attention will keep the connection
between your personal energy and your crystals strong
and clear-flowing, creating a powerful bond and opening
the space for personalised magic to manifest.

ENERGY IS ENERGY IS ENERGY…

A common belief in the crystal world is that crystals easily pick up 'bad' or 'negative' energies, and you should keep others from touching your personal crystals for fear they might get 'contaminated' by your friends' less-than-perfect vibes. However, **energy is simply energy, neither good or bad.** It's human nature to want to assign a characteristic to energy, but in truth, what's considered 'good' by one person might be considered 'bad' by another – it's personal preference. To worry that your crystals need constant cleansing and 'protection' not only keeps you much too focused on the negative (which is not where you want your attention to live), it disregards the innate power and intelligence within crystals themselves. Have faith that your crystals are intelligent beings who can keep themselves clear and high-vibing on their own! If you use crystals for on-body healing – especially in the case of grief or illness - then supporting your crystals with a focused cleanse and charge can indeed be necessary, and your intuition will guide you. And of course, shower your crystals with as much care and attention as you wish – they'll love it! – just remember to always keep your intention behind doing so focused on the positive, rather than the preventative.

MAINTENANCE

Monthly moonbaths (see page 21), especially under a full or new moon, are powerfully recharging for all crystals and are often all that a crystal needs to remain fully charged and activated. Also regularly check that your crystal clusters aren't sitting around covered in a fine layer of dust, as dust reduces the electrostatic charge vital to their crystalline technology. Easily remove dust with a quick water rinse or a small brush (make-up brushes work well).

CRYSTAL PROGRAMMING establishes a very specific intention for a crystal to hold, usually for an energy or result you wish to manifest.

Hold your crystal in both hands and imagine it surrounded by a shimmering ball of golden light. Say aloud the intention which you wish the crystal to hold for you: '**I programme this crystal for** (healing my heart / protecting me while I travel / strengthening my willpower to make healthy food choices). **For the highest good of all, in love and in light.**'

Just remember that you only need to programme a crystal if your intuition clearly guides you to do so. If not, trust that the crystal's magic is already working perfectly for your particular needs and healing!

The process of cleansing and charging your crystals should be as simple or complicated as you feel guided to make it. I personally tend to keep my ritual quite simple: my new crystals usually get a quick Water Cleanse and/or a Breath + Intention Cleanse. I place them on an indoor windowsill to soak up sunlight and moonlight for a day or so, and *voilà*: refreshed, activated, and happy crystals ready to work magic. Simple, quick and very effective!

Have fun experimenting with the following cleansing and charging rituals to discover which feel best for you and your crystals.

WATER

WHY: Water is nature's most potent cleanser and purifier

RITUAL: Rinse your crystal gently under a running tap, or submerge briefly in a bowl of water. If you live near a freshwater source such as a lake or river, it is fantastic to use local, natural water for cleansing: fill a bottle to bring home, or take your crystals out with you to give them the special gift of being cleansed in nature (saltwater can be abrasive so steer clear of ocean and seawater). While water is the easiest way to remove dust and leftover soil, there are many crystals that can dissolve or rust from water exposure so it's important to do your research before cleansing – if in doubt, skip the water and use a different method. To make it easy for you, each crystal's profile clearly lists whether water cleansing is safe.

SUNLIGHT

WHY: Sunlight powerfully shines away stale energies and is an extremely activating force

RITUAL: Most new crystals benefit from at least a short sunbath when you first bring them home: place them in a sunny spot and leave for at least 4 hours. I personally love displaying non-rare crystals such as Amethyst on windowsills as they sparkle so beautifully in the sunlight, but keep in mind that sunlight fades many varieties of crystals over time. If you choose to display your coloured crystal in a sunny spot, you must be at peace with the fact that over time it will transform into a paler, pastel version of itself.

MOONLIGHT

WHY: Moonlight is supercharging and safe for all crystals

RITUAL: There is mysterious magic in moonlight, and crystals thrive on regular moonbaths. Lay your crystals overnight in a place where moonlight will touch them for potent charging; indoor windowsills and tables near a window are the safest option. Many metallic minerals can rust in overnight dew, so use caution with outdoor charging. The light of a new or full moon is especially powerful and supercharging, and moonbaths under these special moons will keep your crystals extra happy and glowingly healthy!

BREATH + INTENTION

WHY: Breath combined with Intention is the easiest and most instant purifying option

RITUAL: Holding your crystal, inhale through your nose, envisioning golden light filling your lungs. Breathe out through your mouth with a gently forceful breath, as though you were blowing out the candles on a birthday cake. Repeat several times until your crystal is visually cleared from dust and/or until you sense that all energy cobwebs have been blown away.

SMOKE

WHY: The cleansing smoke from burning herbs moves and purifies energies

RITUAL: Light your favourite source of herbal smoke and hold your crystal above the stream of smoke, allowing smoke to dance over and around your crystal for several moments. For an extra boost of magic, move the smoking wand around your crystal in a circular motion seven times. Sage bundles and palo santo sticks are popular options, however both are endangered native plants in the wild, so please source them sustainably. A great alternative are bundles of dried local herbs (lavender, rose and cedar are wonderful), and incense sticks are easy and effective.

MUSIC

WHY: Music's vibrational waves harmonise the energy of everything it touches

RITUAL: Chant, ring, drum, strum! Crystals absolutely love being around music, and live music especially brings them to life and infuses them with a special glow. So strum that guitar, chant your mantra, or ring bells and singing bowls near your crystals whenever possible. Don't be shy, they're the most wonderful and non-judgemental audience one could ask for!

EARTH

WHY: 'Earthing' with soil grounds and recharges

RITUAL: Place your crystal on or under the soil in a houseplant, or bury under a few inches of soil in your garden – just don't forget to clearly mark where you left it, many a crystal has returned to the earth this way! Leave for at least one night, or as long as feels right. Earthing is especially good for crystals with grounding properties (Black Tourmaline, Smoky Quartz, etc), and those that have travelled through airport scanners with you. Earthing should not be done with metallic minerals as the water in soil can rust them, or with delicate clusters.

SALT

WHY: Salt is purifying; however, use with caution as it can damage many crystals

RITUAL: Saltwater soaks or burying crystals in salt are traditional cleansing methods, but I don't recommend using salt for general cleansing as it can damage crystals by dulling their shine and weakening clusters. However, if you use your crystals for multiple healing treatments (especially in a spa or massage studio environment), salt can be a quick and effective purifier for keeping your 'worker' crystals fresh. Simply fill a bowl or tray with Himalayan salt (coarse is best as smaller granules can damage clusters) and lay your crystals on top of the salt for at least 10 minutes between sessions.

EVERYDAY MAGIC:
crystallise your life

From sparkling home decor to on-the-go healing
tools, crystals can add magic to every moment of your
daily life. The following suggestions are meant
to spark your own imagination and intuition, so have
fun experimenting – your crystals will guide you!

CRYSTALS + HOME

Your home is so much more than just a very large box of your personal possessions. Whether you're living in your dream abode or a temporary apartment, each room nourishes and supports you in very specific ways. Decorating with crystals transforms your home into a magic-filled sanctuary, and is the easiest way to start crystallising your life. If you're unsure where to display your crystals, simply start by placing them anywhere you would put a decorative candle or houseplant – just be mindful that brightly coloured crystals can fade in direct sunlight. Here are my favourite choices for keeping each room's energy bright and sparkling:

BEDROOM
(for calm sleep + peaceful dreams)
Agate, Amethyst, Black Tourmaline, Celestite, Chalcedony, Danburite, Halite, Lepidolite, Moonstone, Rose Quartz (and for adding heat to bedroom activities try Tangerine Quartz, Carnelian, Garnet, Emerald, Aragonite) *tip: place crystals on your nightstand or under your mattress for healing and guidance while you sleep, and Selenite in closets to clear stagnant energies*

KITCHEN
(for healthy choices + willpower) Amethyst, Apatite, Bloodstone, Carnelian, Clear Quartz, Emerald, Pyrite, Selenite, Shungite *tip: put crystals in your fridge and cupboards to infuse food with extra-healthy vibes*

LIVING + DINING ROOMS
(for communication + relaxation)
Amethyst, Apophyllite, Calcite, Clear Quartz, Desert Rose, Iceland Spar, Selenite, Smoky Quartz, Spirit Quartz, Sulphur *tip: these crystals kept in busy living spaces do double-duty as pretty decor and powerful space clearers*

BATHROOM
(for self-care + health) Agate, Amazonite, Calcite, Celestite, Chalcedony, Chrysocolla, Bloodstone, Emerald, Fluorite, Fuchsite, Jasper *tip: blue and green crystals help transform your bathroom into a healing sanctuary*

CHILDREN'S ROOM
(for calm + angelic protection)
Amethyst, Celestite, Chalcedony, Danburite, Emerald, Lepidolite, Moonstone, Selenite *tip: try Amethyst or Lepidolite under the crib or bed to encourage calm sleep. Make sure to keep crystals away from little mouths!*

CRYSTALS + WORK

Whether you're a self-employed maker or a corporate creative, keeping crystals in your workspace will supercharge your creativity and productivity. Any combo of these crystals is a great place to start:

focus + productivity
Agate, Citrine, Desert Rose, Pyrite, Rainbow Fluorite, Selenite

creativity + inspiration
Amethyst, Ametrine, Aragonite, Clear Quartz, Labradorite, Pyrite, Smoky Quartz, Spirit Quartz

communication
Amazonite, Apophyllite, Celestite, Chrysocolla, Kyanite, Rose Quartz

luck
Amethyst, Citrine, Emerald, Jade, Pyrite, Rutilated Quartz, Sulphur

CRYSTALS ON-THE-GO

Tumbled stones are perfect for keeping crystal magic around while out and about, and most crystal lovers always have at least a few rattling around their handbags, wallets, pockets and cars. You can tuck tumbled stones everywhere from bras to sock cuffs, simply follow your own intuition on what will provide the best support for your upcoming day. Crystal jewellery is also a classic and easy on-the-go option – just remember that your jewellery will also need cleansing and charging from time to time. Sunlight, moonlight, and smoke are the safest methods.

Travel protection: Agate, Amethyst, Black Tourmaline, Bloodstone, Emerald, Hematite, Labradorite, Moonstone, Shungite *tip: Emerald and Moonstone help calm fear of flying. Don't forget to earth cleanse your travel crystals after exposure to airport x-rays*

CRYSTALS + WELLNESS

SLEEP

Absorbing crystal energy while sleeping is extra potent: In addition to keeping crystals placed around your bedroom, small tumbled stones can be easily tucked into your pillowcase, between mattress and boxspring, or laid under your bed for focused healing. Try putting an Amethyst under your head, a Rose Quartz by each side, and a Black Tourmaline by your feet to experience my favourite night time layout. Pay attention to whether some crystals feel too 'active' for your bedroom; I personally can't sleep anywhere near Lapis Lazuli or Tiger's Eye.

BATHE

Add crystals to your bath to transform it into an extra-blissful self-care ritual: If you haven't yet experienced a crystal bath you have something special to look forward to! Tumbled stones are best for baths and make sure not to use crystals that can dissolve or rust, or those containing lead or mercury.

Safe options include Agate, Amethyst, Apatite, Black Tourmaline, Bloodstone, Carnelian, Chalcedony, Citrine, Emerald, Fluorite, Garnet, Hematite, Jade, Jasper, Labradorite, Lepidolite, Moonstone, Rose Quartz, Shungite, Smoky Quartz.

ELIXIRS

Drink your crystals: Giving new meaning to 'on the rocks', a drinkable crystal elixir is liquid (usually water) that has been infused with crystal energy. To make a simple elixir, put one or more small tumbled stones in a glass cup, jar or pitcher filled with filtered or spring water. Place in sunlight or moonlight for at least 12 hours to infuse and charge the water. Remove the crystals and drink up for a lovely internal boost of crystal healing! Try Rose Quartz for love, Amethyst for healing, Citrine for energy, or Shungite for grounding. It is vitally important to use non-toxic stones for elixirs, please do your research before any experimenting!

NOTE: None of the stones listed in this book contain lead or mercury, but it's good to be aware that there are a few crystals out there that do. For example, Galena contains lead, Cinnabar contains mercury.

CRYSTALS + RITUAL

MOON MANIFESTING
Crystals and moon magic are truly a match made in heaven: Besides being the best time to recharge crystals, full and new moons offer supercharged opportunities for manifesting intentions.

NEW MOONS are full of fresh energy, the perfect time for setting new intentions and beginning new projects. A simple yet powerful New Moon + Crystal ritual:
1. Write a list of goals and dreams you wish to manifest
2. Place a Citrine, Tangerine Quartz, Clear Quartz, Garnet, or Moonstone (or combo) on top of your list
3. Leave overnight in the light of the new moon. *Expect miracles.*

FULL MOONS are legendary as the most mysterious and magic-filled night of each month. Emotions and intuitions are heightened, and the curtain between realities is thin. Gratitude rituals are perfect for full moon nights as they are grounding, protective, and possibility expanding:

1. Write a list of the things in your life which fill you with gratitude
2. Place a Labradorite, Amethyst, Pyrite, Selenite, Emerald, or Smoky Quartz (or combo) on top of your list
3. Leave overnight in the light of the full moon. *Expect miracles.*

ALTARS *are prayers in physical form*: Crystals have been used as holy altar objects since ancient times, and all crystal types are appropriate to keep on your personal altar for holding specific intentions, prayers, and wishes.

GRIDDING
There is magic in symmetry: Crystal gridding is the practice of placing crystals in an intentional layout, often following patterns connected to sacred geometry. Crystal gridding can be used both to empower a specific intention and as a mindful meditation practice. Experiment with pre-made patterns or create patterns from your intuition; Pinterest and Instagram are great sources for gridding inspiration, try searching the #crystalgrid hashtag to get started.

CRYSTALS + GIFTS

Crystals are the perfect gifts – they truly never stop giving! Here are my favourite recommendations for a wide variety of occasions:

BIRTHDAY
Amazonite, Amethyst, Apophyllite, Celestite, Citrine, Cobalto Calcite, Fluorite, Rose Quartz, Spirit Quartz

FRIENDSHIP
Agate, Amethyst, Black Tourmaline, Chalcedony, Clear Quartz, Lepidolite, Rose Quartz, Rutilated Quartz, Spirit Quartz, Turquoise

CONGRATULATIONS
Amethyst, Ametrine, Citrine, Fluorite, Pyrite, Spirit Quartz, Sulphur

GRADUATION
Amazonite, Aragonite, Citrine, Emerald, Iceland Spar, Pyrite, Spirit Quartz

NEW JOB
Amazonite, Ametrine, Azurite, Citrine, Emerald, Jade, Pyrite, Fluorite

BRIDAL SHOWER
Amethyst, Apophyllite, Halite, Moonstone, Rose Quartz, Spirit Quartz

WEDDING
Amethyst, Apophyllite, Azurite, Clear Quartz, Rose Quartz, Selenite

NEW HOME
Amethyst, Apophyllite, Black Tourmaline, Halite, Selenite, Smoky Quartz

BABY SHOWER
Amethyst, Celestite, Chalcedony, Chrysocolla, Clear Quartz, Cobalto Calcite, Emerald, Moonstone

NEW MOTHER
Amber, Amethyst, Bloodstone, Carnelian, Celestite, Chrysocolla, Emerald, Garnet, Hematite, Lepidolite, Moonstone, Tangerine Quartz

GET WELL
Amethyst, Apatite, Amber, Aragonite, Bloodstone, Chrysocolla, Emerald, Jasper, Rose Quartz, Sulphur

BROKEN HEART
Black Tourmaline, Danburite, Garnet, Halite, Lepidolite, Rhodonite, Rose Quartz, Rutilated Quartz

GRIEF
Agate, Apache Tears, Chalcedony (pink), Halite, Lepidolite, Malachite, Rhodonite, Rose Quartz, Smoky Quartz

CHAKRAS						
Crown	**3rd Eye**	**Throat**	**Heart**	**Solar Plexus**	**Sacral**	**Root**
MANTRA						
'I know'	'I see'	'I speak'	'I love'	'I share'	'I create'	'I am'
TRADITIONAL COLOUR						
Violet	Indigo	Blue	Green	Yellow	Orange	Red
COMPLIMENTARY COLOUR						
Yellow	Red	Orange	Pink	Violet	Blue	Green

'The gift of healing rests within everyone. It is not a gift given only to a few. It is your birthright as much as it is mine. Everyone can receive healing, and everyone can learn to heal. Everyone can give healing to themselves and others.'

— **Barbara Brennan**, *Light Emerging* (Bantam Books, 1994)

CRYSTALS + CHAKRAS:
you are a rainbow

chakra: from ancient Sanskrit, meaning 'wheel'

MAGIC *Placing crystals directly on specific points of the body activates powerful healing and recharging.*

Our bodies are powered by a vibrant, rainbow-coloured energy system known as *chakras*. First written about over 4000 years ago by holy monks in ancient India, chakras are energy vortexes that vibrate within and around our bodies at specific points. We use our chakras constantly to both draw in and expend energy, and a well-working system is absolutely vital to how healthy you feel both physically and emotionally, as well as how vibrantly you are able to function in your day-to-day life. And if the charging port on your phone looks anything like mine, you won't have a hard time envisioning how necessary it is regularly clear and recharge your chakras (aka your body's charging ports) from the gunk of daily life! Yoga, meditation, and time in nature are great ways to help keep your chakra system healthy, and crystals are potent, easy-to-use tools to add to your chakra health kit – I like to call them chakra vitamins!

You have seven main chakras, running from the bottom of your spine to the top of your head, each associated with a specific colour and energy focus. The chakra vortexes along the front of your body function as delivery systems which move your energy *out* into the world, and the equally important (and often forgotten!) Chakra vortexes along the back of your body *receive* energy and input from your spiritual support staff – a telephone helpline directly to your personal angels and guides.

Crystal chakra healing can manifest in a myriad of ways. You might feel electric tingles or a deep sense of peace, spontaneously break out in tears or laughter, or you may even feel nothing at all. The reaction you're having will always be the 'right' reaction; trust the process, trust your intuition, and trust the intelligence within crystals.

Experiment with the following chakra cleanses to get started using crystals for on-body healing, and don't forget that there are limitless ways to heal with crystals: have fun letting your intuition go ROYGBIV-wild!

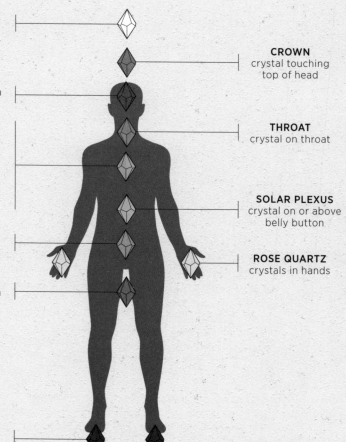

HIGH CROWN
crystal several
inches
above head

CROWN
crystal touching
top of head

3RD EYE
crystal between
eyebrows

THROAT
crystal on throat

HIGH HEART
+
HEART
crystals on
breastbone
(either green
or pink)

SOLAR PLEXUS
crystal on or above
belly button

SACRAL
crystal on
low stomach

ROSE QUARTZ
crystals in hands

ROOT
crystal between
inner thighs

EARTH STAR
crystals
touching feet

Crystal chakra healing

Find a quiet moment and a comfortable place to lie down.
Kick off your shoes and turn your phone to silent. If you wish,
stream calming background music, although silence is equally
powerful. Drink plenty of water before and after.

SIMPLE SINGLE-CHAKRA CLEANSE

This one-stone method is the quickest and easiest way to use crystals for on-body healing. It's great for a quick recharge, applying focused healing to a specific area, or to get to know an individual crystal better (it's great to do this with a new crystal when you first bring it home).

RITUAL Take a crystal and gently roll it between your palms several times to activate it. Place it on the area of its colour-matched chakra – a blue stone on your throat, a green stone on your chest, etc. Breathe deeply, and very simply imagine the crystal radiating its beautiful colour into the area it is touching, the colour spreading and growing more vibrant with each breath you take. If it feels right, repeat the mantra associated with that specific chakra with each breath. You may set an alarm (5 minutes is a great all-purpose amount of time), or simply continue until your intuition tells you that you are done. Don't forget to say thank you to your crystal when you are finished; your gratitude lets it know that you are done charging and unplugs the crystal from your chakra.

Note If a crystal rolls off your body or moves from where you've placed it, take a moment to sense whether it actually needs to be moved back – it may be trying to tell you that its work is done or better used in a slightly different spot. Also, don't forget to give attention to back chakras when working with crystals – traditional chakra colours are based on the front chakra system, experiment using complimentary-coloured crystals on the back of the body (see chart on page 30).

This is a powerful boost for your entire chakra system, great to treat yourself to at least once a week. Modern metaphysics identifies additional chakras beyond the original seven, so this cleanse gives the option of including the modern chakras Earth Star, High Heart, and High Crown.

CRYSTALS NEEDED

Seven crystals, one for each main chakra. For a supercharged experience add:

- 1 Clear Quartz point for the High Crown Chakra
- 2 grounding crystals for the Earth Star Chakra (Black Tourmaline or other black/grey crystal)
- 1 pink crystal for the High Heart Chakra
- 2 Rose Quartz to create a healing cocoon

RITUAL Always start by placing your grounding crystals so that they touch each foot. Begin placing crystals on your body, going in order either from the Root Chakra up, or the Crown Chakra down. The first option is the traditional order (and logistically the easiest option for self-chakra cleansing), but starting at the Crown Chakra and moving down is a powerful variation. Holding a Rose Quartz in each hand, close your eyes and breathe deeply and calmly. Imagine the crystals beginning to glow from the inside. Their colours start radiating outwards, expanding with each breath to fill the entire room with a shimmering bubble of rainbow colour. Breathe this rainbow in and imagine it rushing through your veins, purifying and energising every cell. Exhale and imagine the shimmering colour exhaling out of your nose and mouth in a beautiful rainbow cloud. *You are a rainbow.* Take at least 10 minutes to experience the potent magic of a complete crystal chakra healing. When finished, remove the crystals in the opposite order from which you placed them, unplugging your energy from each crystal by thanking each one individually. **You are healed, you are whole, you are light!**

MEDITATE

Quiet contemplation with your crystals
will help you deepen your connection with
them and gain your own crystal insights.
Try meditating with a crystal in your non-
dominant hand, on your heart, or on your
third eye (between your eyebrows). Gently
observe any sensations and shifts you
might feel in your body and emotions
as you connect and bond more
deeply with your crystal.

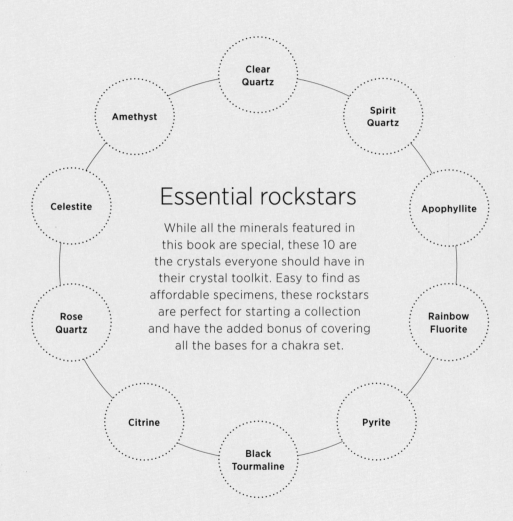

Clear Quartz

Spirit Quartz

Amethyst

Apophyllite

Celestite

Essential rockstars

While all the minerals featured in this book are special, these 10 are the crystals everyone should have in their crystal toolkit. Easy to find as affordable specimens, these rockstars are perfect for starting a collection and have the added bonus of covering all the bases for a chakra set.

Rainbow Fluorite

Rose Quartz

Pyrite

Citrine

Black Tourmaline

#Goals

Psst... The 'goal' of working with crystals isn't to magically conjure up a perfect life for ourselves – the perfect romance, body, career, bank account... These are all great things to have, but focusing on them is missing out on the source of true happiness, and the point of this whole 'being a human' experience. Instead, the greatest magic to be gained from working with crystals (and from all forms of 'self-help', really) is that it supports you in becoming the clearest, shiniest, most inspired and grounded version of yourself. So that you can form a deep reservoir of well-being from which to share your unique kindness, caring and love with everyone your life touches. **Less self-help, more everyone-help.** Because that, dear crystal friends, is what it's all really about. *Radiate kindness, compassion and love, and I promise that the 'perfect' life you desire will be all yours.*

#beagoodhuman

THE CRYSTALS

THE **A–Z GUIDE**

✳ **Colour** variations

◎ Largest modern **source(s)**

⚜ **Chakra(s)** crystal resonates to

♡ **Special care** recommendations

💧 Whether **water exposure** causes damage

Magic = Metaphysical qualities

Notes = Practical information

Agate

PROTECTION + COURAGE + STRENGTH + GROUNDING

✳ **Colour** All shades of the rainbow

◔ **Born in** Worldwide

♨ **Chakra** Varies according to colour

◌ **Water Cleansing** ☒ Y ☐ N

MAGIC Agate is a protective mineral with ancient stories to tell. This multicoloured, banded gemstone has been carved into holy objects and magic amulets since first discovered, thousands of years ago, on the banks of the Greek river Achates. Legends have long foretold that Agate can grant powers of invisibility and courage. *Invisibility = much more than only what meets the eye*, and Agate is a stone to keep close whenever you feel vulnerable or in need of extra protection, both physically and emotionally. Although your journey through life will hold many moments for shining brightly in the spotlight, it will also offer equally important opportunities for walking bravely through shadows, both internal and external. Agate, with its mix of brightly translucent and darkly opaque bands, reminds us that being a true magic-maker requires stepping bravely into both situations – the light *and* the dark – and will help support and protect you along the many turns in your journey as a Lightworker.

NOTES Agate is a banded variety of the mineral Chalcedony, its distinctive layers best shown off once cut or polished. Slices or geodes with sparkling 'drusy' at the centre (a coating of tiny crystals, pictured) are easy to find and a classic favourite. Agate is found throughout the world in a vast array of colour combinations, with many varieties named after their source location. Agate is an Ayurvedic birthstone for May, and a zodiac birthstone for Capricorn and Gemini.

Amazonite

TRUTH-TELLING + FLOW + INSPIRATION

❋ **Colour** Bright blue-green
⊘ **Born in** USA, Madagascar, Russia, Brazil
⬡ **Chakra** Throat
◌ **Water Cleansing** ☒ Y ☐ N

MAGIC *Speak your truth*. Amazonite encourages you in your quest to be a brave and fearless truth-teller. Like the powerful river after which this opaque crystal is named, Amazonite is a stone of flow, strength, and adventure. Encouraging you to dig deep and mine your murky depths for shining truths and inspirations, this truth-teller talisman is a valuable crystal ally for singers, actors, teachers, writers, and anyone who communicates for either a living or passion. Hold Amazonite up to your throat chakra for a few moments before that big audition or presentation, or tuck a small piece into your clothing to accompany you for in-the-moment inspiration. An essential crystal for all you social media mavens who feel led to inspire and uplift, Amazonite will guide you to bravely post and share from your higher self for a Light-filled social media presence. *More inspiration, less aspiration*. Because when we encourage others to fly, we are also lifted higher – let Amazonite help you bravely share your truth so that we can all soar together!

NOTES Amazonite is generally found as large, non-crystallised pieces, although tabular crystal formations are also possible. It is commonly sold both in raw and polished form, both equally beautiful and powerful. Amazonite embedded with Smoky Quartz and/or Black Tourmaline, a common combination, has an added boost of grounding energy.

THE CRYSTALS

Amber

IMMUNE-BOOSTING + SOOTHING
+ FOLKLORIC MAGIC

✳ **Colour** Honey-orange + yellow

◎ **Born in** Baltic Sea region

♋ **Chakras** Sacral, Heart, Solar Plexus

◌ **Water Cleansing** ☒ Y ☐ N

MAGIC Amber is a stone of ancient forest magic and old-world fairytales. Born from the 'blood' of prehistoric pine trees, these honey-coloured gems are fossilised drops of resin which have been smoothed and polished by saltwater waves over millions of years. This is a valuable crystal friend for those with ancestral roots in Eastern Europe, the traditional homeland of Amber; spend time with this glowing stone to connect with the myths and folklore of your ancestors, and to awaken the indigenous magic and wisdom that runs deep within your being. In contrast to the snowy landscape from which it hails, Amber is a deeply warming stone, and has been treasured since prehistoric times for its healing and pain-relieving abilities. To heal with Amber, try placing a piece on your sacral chakra to release inherited ancestral karmas; on your solar plexus chakra for a burst of sunshine vitality and healing; and/or on your heart chakra to wrap your immune system and heart in a giant, warm-honey hug.

NOTES Although the Baltic Sea region is the main source for Amber, specimens also come from Central America – Spanish conquistadors told tales of Montezuma, the Aztec emperor, stirring his chocolate with an amber spoon. Watch out for convincing plastic imitations; real Amber warms easily and releases a piney smell when rubbed, as well as floats in salted water, unlike imitators. Look closely, Amber sometimes has prehistoric insects trapped inside!

Amethyst

TRANSFORMATION + PROTECTION
+ ADDICTION-RELEASE + SLEEP AID

✳ **Colour** Shades of lavender + violet
🍥 **Born in** Brazil, Uruguay, Worldwide
🐚 **Chakra** Crown
♡ **Care** Fades in direct sunlight
◊ **Water Cleansing** ☒ Y ☐ N

MAGIC *Transcend to Transform*. Treasured by countless generations of crystal lovers, Amethyst's name comes from an Ancient Greek legend involving the playboy god Bacchus, a pure maiden named Amethyst, and way too much wine... Taking legend to heart, Ancient Greeks and Romans drank from Amethyst-studded goblets as a talisman against overindulgence and addiction. Today, Amethyst reminds us to always treat body and mind as a sacred temple. It helps us unplug from unhealthy attachments, and powerfully cleanses body, mind and aura from negative or addictive patterns. A stone of protection, Amethyst creates an ultraviolet bubble of protective light around people and spaces, and is very helpful for insomnia and nightmares. A stone of transcendence, Amethyst heightens psychic powers, and will strengthen your connection to all things mystical and magical. One of my Essential Rockstars, Amethyst is a truly miraculous crystal that blesses everyone and everything within its wide energy field.

NOTES At one time as rare and expensive as diamonds, Amethyst is believed to get its purple hue from inclusions of iron and aluminium, although how this quartz's colour is created remains a bit of a scientific mystery. Individual crystals are found worldwide, while the majority of clusters on the market come from Brazil and Uruguay. Amethyst is a traditional and Ayurvedic birthstone for February, and a zodiac birthstone for Aquarius and Pisces.

Ametrine

CONFIDENCE + INTUITION + MANIFESTATION + GOALS

✴ **Colour** Mix of violet + orange

⊘ **Born in** Bolivia, Brazil

🜨 **Chakras** Solar Plexus, Crown

♡ **Care** Fades in direct sunlight

◊ **Water Cleansing** ☒ Y ☐ N

MAGIC The cosmic love child of Amethyst and Citrine, Ametrine is a stone for dance-to-your-own-beat creativity. Combining crown and solar plexus chakra energies together in one crystal, this violet-orange rock is all about taking charge of your own life and staying true to your intuition. Ametrine helps you commit to living a life filled with things from your 'must' list, instead of from other people's 'should' lists; throw off those shackles of conformity and begin manifesting your magnificent, beyond-the-ordinary dreams and visions! Ametrine = follow *your* dreams.

The combination of Citrine's motivational powers with Amethyst's vibration of wholeness and transcendence also makes Ametrine a great partner for sticking to goals, clearing bad habits, and kicking addictions. Try drinking an elixir of Ametrine to help you stay on track with health goals, sleep with one under your pillow for dreamtime support, and keep one in view while studying or working for an extra zap of brainpower, focus and inspiration.

NOTES Ametrine specimens are generally mostly violet-coloured, with small sections of orange. Bolivia is the main source of natural Ametrine. Although specimens from other localities are often heat-treated to enhance their orange colour, you will find these enhanced stones still have a powerful metaphysical vibration.

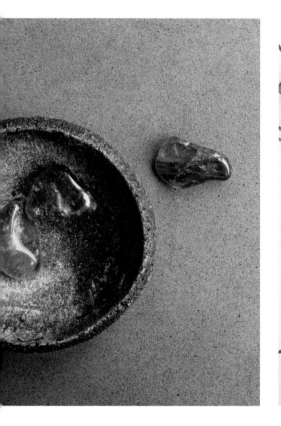

BLUE

Apatite

WILLPOWER + HEALTHY CHOICES + DETOX

✳ **Colour** Teal blue

◔ **Born in** Brazil, India

◔ **Chakras** 3rd Eye, Throat

◌ **Water Cleansing** ☒ Y ☐ N

MAGIC *Rock Your Willpower*. Blue Apatite is the crystal to grab whenever you need help with anything willpower-related: resolutions, healthy eating, substance avoidance, self-kindness, etc. Keep one of these teal-blue rocks within view in your kitchen to help you consistently make healthy, nourishing choices. This lovely stone works by detoxing you from patterns and habits which aren't helpful, the deep-rooted stuff holding on from past lives and alternate realities which you definitely want to release for present clarity and health. Take a bath with Apatite to infuse your water with detoxing, health-supporting vibes, or try drinking an Apatite water elixir for healthy infusions from the inside out. This is a great stone for bedrooms, as it will gently work on you while you sleep. Remember: being healthy isn't a self-serving goal, as the better you feel, the better you can share your gifts and passions with the world.

NOTES Apatite forms in a variety of colours, with the blue variety being the most widely available and affordable. Sometimes sold under the name Teal Apatite, Blue Apatite is available both as expensive transparent crystals and affordable tumbled stones. Apatite was named by the Ancient Greeks after Apate, goddess of deceit, as it was often mistaken for other minerals, most commonly Fluorite and Aquamarine.

Apophyllite

SPACE CLEARING + ENERGY FILTER
+ 3RD EYE AWAKENING

✳ **Colour** Crystal clear, mint green

◎ **Born in** India

☯ **Chakras** 3rd Eye, Crown

◌ **Water Cleansing** ☒ Y ☐ N

MAGIC *PURIFY.* Apophyllite is the 'air purifier' of the crystal kingdom, continuously filtering large amounts of energy to keep vibrations fresh, sparkling clear, and extremely high-vibe. Place a cluster in areas with busy energetic traffic such as living rooms, hallways and kitchens, and within 24 hours you should definitely notice a positive difference in the quality of that space's energy. This is an essential crystal for healing practitioners to keep in waiting and treatment rooms for energy purifying, and transmutation. Apophyllite crystal tips are a popular option for expanding third eye awareness and focus; meditate with one of these small, pyramid-shaped crystals between your eyebrows to enhance your ability to be fair, balanced, and

spiritually awake in all your interactions. One of my Essential Rockstars for its energy-purifying abilities, Apophyllite helps facilitate conscious communication and transforms judgement, making this a perfect crystal gift for new homes, new marriages, and new businesses. Clusters with peachy-pink *Stilbite*, an easy-to-find combo, fill spaces and people with heart-opening, joyful vibrations.

NOTES Apophyllite is one of the best bang-for-your-buck crystals, as stunning large clusters are more affordable than most other mineral clusters of similar size and sparkle. It most commonly forms as a clear, colourless mineral mixed with a variety of opaque 'zeolite' minerals, including Stilbite and Heulandite. Green Apophyllite is a rarer and more expensive variety (avoid green-dyed imitations!). Apophyllite crystal tips can 'pop' off, leaving a flat (but still beautiful) surface, so use care to keep your cluster's tips intact.

STAR

Aragonite

CHANGE + EMBRACING THE UNKNOWN + GROUNDING

✺ **Colour** Burnt orange, white
◎ **Born in** Morocco, Spain, USA
♋ **Chakras** Sacral, Root
⬡ **Water Cleansing** ☐ Y ☒ N

MAGIC *When one door closes, another one opens*. Star Aragonite, with its dense core radiating starry spikes in all directions, helps you stay open to a sense of adventure and curiosity as change swirls around you. Change is inevitable, something that – without any doubt – is coming down the road for all of us. Instead of clinging tightly to the past, let Aragonite help you embrace the unknown and its myriad of possibilities, adventures, and opportunities. This is a great crystal ally for times when world news and events overwhelm, making you feel like crawling into a hole and sleeping for the next decade (or so). These are the times when your light is needed more than ever, my Lightworker friend, so let Aragonite help you stay sharp, engaged, and focused on the bigger picture. Lie with a crystal on your sacral chakra, breathe calmly and deeply, and meditate on these wise words from none other than Marilyn Monroe, supreme goddess of sensual sacral energy: *'Sometimes good things fall apart so better things can fall together.'*

NOTES A calcium-based mineral, Aragonite is a harder and denser form of Calcite. It forms in a variety of shapes and colours, with star clusters being the most eye-catching and popular form. These are often referred to as Sputnik Aragonite, as their spiky crystals bear a resemblance to the Soviet-era satellites.

Aura Quartz

FUN + MAGIC + PLAYFULNESS + CREATIVITY

✳ **Colour** Iridescent rainbow shades
◉ **Born in** USA, China
༄ **Chakras** Varies according to colour
💧 **Water Cleansing** ☒ Y ☐ N

MAGIC Aura crystals are the party kids of the modern crystal revival. Immensely popular, these fun crystals first came on the scene in the '80s and are a combination of natural and man-made alchemies. Beginning their lives as natural clear quartz points or clusters, they are treated with a combination of extremely high heat and vaporised precious metals to create their distinctive rainbow-shimmer coating and saturated colouring. Besides looking like unicorn tears made real, Aura Quartz's main gift lies in being a visual reminder of the magic that comes from keeping a sense of child-like playfulness and open-minded curiosity. Keep this crystal within view to provide a daily reminder to not take life (or yourself!) too seriously,

and to *never, ever stop believing in the possibility of magic!*

NOTES As treated crystals are currently riding a wave of popularity, manufacturers have begun experimenting with coating a variety of crystals with iridescence, including Spirit Quartz, Amethyst clusters and Aragonite. If the word 'aura' is attached to a crystal, assume that it has a man-made coating. Quality aura crystals have a coating that cannot be scratched off; avoid cheap imitations that scratch easily as they are coated with chemicals rather than precious metals. The specific names of aura crystals can get a little confusing, as there are many variations and overlaps as well as new varieties being created. Classic favourites include white or clear *Angel Aura* (pictured, also called Opal Aura), multicoloured *Titanium Aura* (pictured), bright blue *Aqua Aura*, and blue-purple *Indigo Aura* (also called Tanzan Aura).

Azurite

ILLUMINATION + SERENITY + STRESS RELIEF

✳ **Colour** Royal azure blue
⊘ **Born in** Morocco, Mexico
❧ **Chakras** 3rd Eye, Throat
◇ **Water Cleansing** ☐ Y ☒ N

MAGIC Azurite is a stone of powerful third eye illuminations and insights. A special crystal of awareness and expansion, place Azurite between your eyebrows for a zap of clarity and serenity whenever you feel overwhelmed. Inhale deeply, and exhale out a grey storm cloud of your worries, indecisions and fears, watching them gently float away over a calm, royal-blue sea of Azurite awareness and clarity. *Gentle peace, deep serenity*. Wonderful for clearing your energy after difficult conversations or emotional outbursts, simply hold a crystal to your throat or third eye to help you recentre

and rebalance. Just having a piece of deep blue Azurite in your presence helps melt old grudges, outdated beliefs, and limiting fears from your psyche and aura. Azurite asks you to rise up and be your best self at all times, helping you remain calm and grounded as you work through your personal triggers and edges, guiding you towards true inner tranquility. *Azurite = Keep Calm And Rock On.*

NOTES Azurite has more than 150 different crystal formations, from 'mossy' drusy crystals on rock (pictured) to expensive crystal clusters with such intense saturation that their blue colour can only be seen when held up to a light source. Polished pieces usually also contain swirls of bright green Malachite, adding a grounded heart energy to Azurite's metaphysical gifts.

Bloodstone

COURAGE + MYSTICISM + DETOX + PROTECTION

✷ **Colour** Dark green with flecks of red

☿ **Born in** India, Myanmar, Canada

☙ **Chakras** Root, Sacral, Heart

💧 **Water Cleansing** ☒ Y ☐ N

MAGIC *Middle Earth. Hogwarts. Westeros.* If you know and love at least one of these realms, mythical Bloodstone is most likely a magic-filled talisman for you. A stone of many legends, Bloodstone was known as 'Martyr's Stone' in the Middle Ages, a favourite for Christian jewellery and carvings as it was believed to represent the blood of Christ on green moss. Modern-day mystics prize this stone for its strengthening and grounding gifts, as well as its ability to open portals to the elemental realm of elves, gnomes, and fairies. *Commune with this stone to tap into your inner magician.* Also possessing a wonderful ability to strengthen your body's circulation and eliminate toxins, this is a great crystal to keep around when you're cleansing, detoxing, or just recovering from a late night out. Bloodstone creates a protective aura around you, so tuck a piece into your pocket, bra or bag on days when you need an extra-special boost of courage and protection *aka* when you need some Gandalf-Dumbledore wizardry on your side!

NOTES Bloodstone is a form of Chalcedony speckled with red spots of iron oxide. In antiquity, it was known as Heliotrope, which is still occasionally used as an alternate name. Bloodstone is a traditional and Ayurvedic birthstone for March, and a zodiac birthstone for Aries.

Calcite

HEALING + ANGELIC GUIDANCE + ENERGY AMPLIFIER

✳ **Colour** All shades of the rainbow
◉ **Born in** Worldwide
♋ **Chakra** Varies according to colour
💧 **Water Cleansing** ☐ Y ☒ N

MAGIC Calcite is a healing mineral, encouraging softness and receptivity by gently opening our hearts to radiant well-being and angelic guidance. This is a great stone for *distance healing*, the gift of sending love and support to others. To do this, sit in a quiet place holding a piece of Calcite. Bring an image of the person into your mind. Imagine a golden or pink light surrounding them, enveloping them in a glowing, loving bubble. Don't project specific outcomes or wishes, just love on them, bathing them in your care and support. *Be the healer and be healed*. An energy amplifier, Calcite can often be spotted as little white or clear crystals formed on clusters of other minerals, adding an energy-enhancing booster shot to the other mineral's powers. *Honey Calcite* (pictured) is an extremely soothing variety, especially great for colds, hangovers, cramps, and upset stomachs. Place one on your belly and relax as its warm, healing vibes spread through you. Try this in combo with a warm mug of lemon-ginger-honey tea for ultra-nourishing comfort and healing. *Pink Mangano Calcite*, another favourite variety, is a must for its Reiki-enhancing gifts.

NOTES Calcite forms worldwide in an amazing multitude of colours and clusters. From unique varieties such as Cobalto and Iceland Spar (given their own feature in this book), to a variety of tumbled stones and sparkling geodes, Calcite is an abundant and generally affordable mineral.

Carnelian

ENERGY + CONFIDENCE + CREATIVITY + VITALITY

✳ **Colour** Fiery shades of orange, red, brown
◎ **Born in** Brazil, India, Uruguay
❧ **Chakras** Sacral, Root, Solar Plexus
◊ **Water Cleansing** ☒ Y ☐ N

MAGIC *Smoke alert:* Carnelian gets inner fires burning hot and bright! Fire-coloured Carnelian's gifts lie in igniting energising flames under you in a myriad of magical ways. Lacking the energy and focus to bring your creative daydreams into reality? Carnelian. Could your confidence as a vibrant, sexy creature use a major boost? Carnelian. Bedroom activities need some new spice? Carnelian! This crystal makes a great gift for people preparing for or healing from a major physical accomplishment (childbirth, surgery, marathon, etc.), and also very helpful for energising more modest physical goals aka

finally committing to that exercise routine. Bring Carnelian to the gym for a pocket-sized personal trainer who will always encourage you to do your very best! Carnelian is immune-boosting, so keep it close during cold and flu season, and little pieces kept in kitchen cupboards and fridges are great for adding extra vitality to your food. Prized by everyone from the Ancient Egyptians to Napoleon for good reason, add some Carnelian into your life and get ready to shine brightly!

NOTES Carnelian is a variety of Chalcedony, found only in 'massive' (non-crystallized) form. One of the oldest gemstones to be polished for use as jewellery and talismans, Carnelian is a historical birthstone for August, and a traditional birthstone for Virgo.

Celestite

CALM + INTUITION + SERENDIPITY + ANGELIC INSPIRATION

Colour Powdery blue

Born in Madagascar

Chakras Throat, Crown

Care Fades in direct sunlight

Water Cleansing ☐ Y ☒ N

MAGIC Heavenly-blue Celestite clusters are sparkling gifts of angelic intuition. Connecting you with personal guidance from the heavens, Celestite strengthens your trust in gut instincts, inspirations, and magical serendipity. Keep a cluster of this beautiful crystal by your bedside and you will be gifted with transformative messages and guidance from your angels during dream-time. One of the most soothing and peace-filled crystals, Celestite is magic at calming stress and anxiety. Are you one of those people who can't stop overthinking everything? Having Celestite around will help you transform those perfectionist tendencies and lighten up on your self-limiting habits of over-analysing ***everything*** (Virgos, this crystal is a must-have for you!). A cluster on your desk provides workday inspiration and creative breakthroughs. One of my Essential Rockstars, Celestite's special brand of angelic magic truly is a gift sent from heaven!

NOTES Celestite is most commonly found in the form of a 'geode', a round rock with a hollow centre lined with crystals. When broken open, Celestite geodes reveal sparkling masses of tabular, light blue crystals. A softer mineral, Celestite should be handled with care as crystals can be easily damaged. Keep in a shaded spot and charge only in moonlight, as sunlight will cause Celestite to fade over time. Celestine is a common alternative name.

BLUE + PINK

Chalcedony

STRESS RELIEF + SELF-CARE + HEALING + SOOTHING

Colour Pastel blue or pink

Born in Brazil, Malawi, Namibia

Chakras Throat, Heart

Water Cleansing ☒ Y ☐ N

MAGIC Chalcedony's energy is like a soothing lullaby encapsulated in a crystal. One of the most calming members of the crystal kingdom, these gently luminous minerals are stones of inner peace and cosmic self-care. Pastel-coloured Chalcedony helps you to intentionally commit time and space for *caring for yourself*, channelling healing and inner radiance to replace stress and burnout. A powerful anti-inflammatory for both mind and spirit, hold a polished stone whenever you need a moment of peace. Gently run your fingers over Chalcedony's silky-smooth surface and breathe deeply, imagining yourself surrounded by a sweetly nurturing bubble of pink or blue light. A piece under the pillow banishes nightmares and restless sleep, and Blue Chalcedony is an especially good sleep aid for children's rooms and nurseries (*Blue Lace Agate*, a variety of Chalcedony, is equally soothing). Both blue and pink varieties awaken your inner child, helping you to live life with a sense of child-like wonder, bright-eyed optimism, and hope-filled light heartedness.

NOTES Chalcedony is a variety of microcrystalline quartz (quartz composed of miniscule crystals) which is snowy white in its pure state. The addition of metal elements transforms Chalcedony into a wide variety of minerals, including Agates and Jaspers. Chalcedony forms in a variety of colours with a range of metaphysical attributes. Pastel blue and pink are the most soothing varieties, and are commonly available as small tumbled stones, great for healing baths and elixirs. Chalcedony is a traditional birthstone for May, and a zodiac birthstone for Capricorn and Gemini.

Chrysocolla

EMPOWERED FEMININITY + GRACE + INTUITION + TRUTH

✵ **Colour** Turquoise blue

◉ **Born in** Mexico, USA

☍ **Chakra** Throat

◌ **Water Cleansing** ☒ Y ☐ N
Polished pieces only

MAGIC You know those women who make you feel nurtured, inspired – *alive* – just by being in their presence? Who light up an entire room with their inner glow? If you're drawn to embodying a transcendent, empowered form of feminine energy – or you crave being surrounded by powerful women – Chrysocolla is a stone for you. Activating the Divine Feminine in all of us, this bright blue mineral will help you speak your truth with grace, wisdom and power. From Christianity's nurturing Mother Mary to gentle Kuan Yin, Buddhist goddess of compassion, and from sensual Oshun, Yoruba goddess of love, to fierce, take-no-bullshit Kali, Hindu goddess of destruction and dissolution, empowered femininity takes many forms and faces within our religions and mythologies. *Every single human can benefit from nurturing the feminine aspects of their intuition and power*. Traditionally a stone associated with hermits and monks, Chrysocolla is also a supportive gift for stay-at-home parents to help lift depression or anxiety stemming from a sense of isolation. Clusters mixed with green Malachite, a common combo, are potent stones swirling with both Divine Masculine and Feminine magic.

NOTES Chrysocolla's blue-green colouring is created from oxidised copper. This soft mineral is often found in deposits with other copper-based stones such as green Malachite or blue Azurite. Chrysocolla forms in a variety of shapes, from delicate velvety pieces (pictured), to more durable specimens that can withstand polishing.

Citrine

ENERGY + GOAL-SETTING + ABUNDANCE + LUCK + CREATIVITY

✳ **Colour** Bright orange
◉ **Born in** Brazil, The Congo, Madagascar
♨ **Chakra** Solar Plexus
♡ **Care** Fades in direct sunlight
◊ **Water Cleansing** ☒ Y ☐ N

MAGIC *Take your Vitamin C(itrine)!* Sunshine encapsulated in a crystal, Citrine supercharges your solar plexus chakra to help you manifest your wildest dreams into reality. Have a stack of goals, dreams, and to-do lists to conquer? Try this Citrine meditation, useful for everyone from Type A super-achievers to daydreamers who struggle with follow-through: Hold a piece of Citrine in your hands, or lay one on your navel, and imagine a specific goal from either your wishlist or to-do list. Place that goal in a clear balloon and let it hang a few feet in front of you. Imagine energising flames beginning to emerge from your Citrine crystal, flickering upwards and outwards, slowly changing the colour of the balloon from clear to a golden, fiery orange. With a puff, blow that shimmering balloon up and away, to the land where dreams always come true and to-do lists are always finished on time. *Manifesting magic!* One of my Essential Rockstars, Citrine is a classic stone of prosperity and luck, and a must-have for workspaces and offices to keep creative ideas flowing brightly and abundantly.

NOTES The fiery orange Citrine most know and love is actually Amethyst that has been heated at high temperatures, which transforms it from purple to orange. Citrine does occur naturally in the earth's crust, but natural specimens are uncommon, expensive and often a dull, opaque yellow-brown. Both heat-treated and natural Citrine hold strong magic – try to get your hands on both to feel the energy differences between them.

Cobalto Calcite

JOY + LOVE + POSITIVE ENERGY

✷ **Colour** Bright shades of pink + fuschia

◎ **Born in** Morocco, The Congo

🜨 **Chakra** Heart

♡ **Care** Fades in direct sunlight

💧 **Water Cleansing** ☐ Y ☒ N

MAGIC It's no accident that this crystal is the colour of Valentine hearts and roses, as this is one joyful, love-filled rock! Hot pink Cobalto Calcite is less common than its paler pink sister-in-love, Rose Quartz, but is definitely worth seeking out to add a bright spark of happiness to your home and spirit. Nurturing openness and emotional intelligence, Cobalto Calcite helps you remember how to love with a sense of lightness and delight. Clusters with dots and ribbons of bright green Malachite are a special blend of both heart chakra colours, adding an extra layer of compassion into the heart-nourishing experience this crystal offers. Cobalto Calcite is a wonderful companion for times when your confidence lags, your energy is low, or you simply need a reminder that life is best experienced through hot pink-coloured glasses. Hold this crystal up to your heart whenever you need a quick, effervescent boost of cheerful vibes and vitality!

NOTES Cobalto Calcite is a form of Calcite. Its colour come from the chemical element cobalt, and it most commonly forms as tiny drusy crystals on a hard rock matrix, creating what looks like sparkling pink moss on dark rock. Lots of common name variations exist for this crystal including Cobalt, Cobaltoan and Cobaltian Calcite.

PINK

Danburite

ANGELIC SERENITY + NURTURING + SLEEP AID

✳ **Colour** Pale pink
◎ **Born in** Mexico
🜁 **Chakras** Heart, Crown
♡ **Care** Fades in direct sunlight
◇ **Water Cleansing** ☒ Y ☐ N

MAGIC Like a gentle embrace, Pink Danburite wraps you in a cocoon of comforting, nurturing love. This is a wonderful crystal for when days are grey and you just really need a hug. Heart-soothing Danburite holds a tender 'mothering' energy, but without any complicated history attached – remember those simple days of childhood when a hug from a parent could magically make everything okay? Danburite holds that special energy of child-like innocence and trust. And if you never had the experience of nurturing, supportive parenting, Danburite also holds a safe space for healing your inner child.

This is an important crystal ally for those who haven't received enough loving care, both in childhood and adulthood, and also for those grieving the loss of a parent. Deeply soothing to the nervous system, Danburite is a great crystal remedy if you have trouble sleeping. Place a crystal on your bedside table, and Danburite will join your heart and crown chakras to connect you with the angelic realm, gently wafting you up to new heights of higher consciousness and serenity.

NOTES Danburite forms in unusual crystal 'blades' up to 30 centimetres (1 foot) in length, with tips often crystallised in a wedge shape, similar to topaz crystals. It forms in shades of white and yellow in addition to pink, however pink specimens are considered to be the most metaphysically active. Danburite is a softer mineral and chips easily, so use with care.

Desert Rose

MEDITATION + GROUNDING + FOCUS + GRIEF

✵ **Colour** Sandy brown

◎ **Born in** Mexico, Morocco

♋ **Chakras** Root, Crown, Sacral

◇ **Water Cleansing** ☐ Y ☒ N

MAGIC Formed from ancient desert sand, Desert Rose is a sandy form of the mineral Selenite and holds many of the same cleansing properties, with an added boost of grounding energy. Have a hard time sitting still or focusing? Desert Rose offers you the gift of balance and focused calm, making this a great crystal for desks, workspaces, and anywhere you need access to clarity, focus, and concentration. One of my favorite crystals for meditation and yoga spaces, Desert Rose vibrates with a uniquely aligning blend of root and crown chakra energies, creating a simultaneously grounding/uplifting vibration that anyone near it can easily tap into. Desert Rose also helps gently support those processing grief, especially grief related to miscarriage or the death of a family member or pet. Lie with a crystal on your low stomach to help you process, heal, and transform. Holding a quiet strength on the masculine spectrum of energies, this is a crystal many men and young boys resonate with, and a Desert Rose can be a wonderfully grounding and supportive gift for the special guys in your life.

NOTES Desert Rose forms as bladed clusters arranged in the shape of a rosette, in varying shades of brown and tan. Some specimens release a dusting of sand when touched and can erode easily, so handle with care. It is also commonly called Selenite Rose or Gypsum Rose.

Emerald

ABUNDANCE + LUCK + HEALTH + PROTECTION

✳ **Colour** Emerald green with swirls of black + white

◈ **Born in** Colombia, Zambia, Brazil

♋ **Chakras** Heart, Sacral

◇ **Water Cleansing** ☒ Y ☐ N

MAGIC Emeralds have shone brightly through countless mythologies and histories for good reason. Powerful humans from King Solomon to Cleopatra to Elizabeth Taylor have famously rocked these sparkling green jewels, and they chose wisely – this is a gemstone that can manifest huge gifts of magnetic good fortune, abundance, and health. A crystal of springtime fertility and vitality, the Ancient Egyptians used Emerald magic for everything from youthfulness and healthy childbirth to protection in the afterlife. The Egyptians had the right idea: meditate with Emerald on your heart or sacral chakras to tap into unlimited abundance, vitality, fertility and health, and add it to your bath to infuse your entire body with healing energies. Extremely protective, this is a good stone to take on the road with you as a talisman for safe travel, and it can bring calm to fearful flyers. Emerald is a nurturing, protective crystal for every room of the house.

NOTES Although gemstone-quality Emeralds are famously pricey, Emeralds in tumbled stone form are easy to find and inexpensive. Unlike gemstones, these tumbled Emeralds are opaque green with white and black inclusions. Emerald is a traditional birthstone for May, and a zodiac birthstone for Taurus and Cancer.

RAINBOW

Fluorite

FOCUS + PRODUCTIVITY + CREATIVITY
+ ANTI-INFLAMMATORY

- ✳ **Colour** Bands of green, purple, blue, white
- ⌖ **Born in** Mexico, China
- � **Chakras** Heart, Throat, Crown
- ♡ **Care** Fades in direct sunlight
- ◊ **Water Cleansing** ☒ Y ☐ N

MAGIC *Rock Your Genius.* Bestowed with the nickname 'Genius Stone' by medieval alchemists, Rainbow Fluorite is a crystal of focus, clear-thinking and inspiration. A 'cooling' crystal, Fluorite helps decrease inflammation in both mind and body: soak in a bath with tumbled stones to reduce bodily pain, tensions and infections (great for getting over a cold!), and carry a piece with you to stay calm and cool-headed during daily life. If you struggle with concentration or hyperactivity, this multicoloured stone helps clear mental fog and disorganisation, making it a fantastic crystal ally for study, work and general productivity (Fluorite is very happy living on a desk or in a workspace!). Fluorite's chakra resonance changes according to a specimen's dominant colour; mostly green crystals have a heart-calming and throat-opening energy, while those with more purple are aligned with the crown chakra. One of my Essential Rockstars for its unparalleled gifts of inspiration and focus, bring some Fluorite magic into your life and get ready to dazzle the world with your inner genius!

NOTES Fluorite spans the widest colour range in the mineral kingdom, from colourless to bright shades of pink and yellow. 'Rainbow' Fluorite (a mix of green, purple, blue, white) is most commonly sold in polished form to highlight its beautiful colour bands, although raw specimens also have a lovely energy. Cubic Fluorite clusters of green or purple hold a similar energy to Rainbow Fluorite.

Fuchsite

FAIRIES + NATURE + HERBALISM + HOLISTIC HEALTH

- ✳ **Colour** Shimmering green
- ⦿ **Born in** Brazil
- ⬡ **Chakra** Heart
- ♡ **Care** Fades in direct sunlight
- ◇ **Water Cleansing** ☐ Y ☒ N

MAGIC A gentle heart crystal connected to the elemental kingdom of fairies, nature angels and earth spirits, Fuchsite helps channel wisdom from the fairy realm, especially insights related to plants, herbal remedies and holistic healing. Shimmering Fuchsite makes a perfect gift for the gardeners in your life, and is a wonderful addition to your personal crystal toolkit to increase your green thumb and connection to plants and nature. While this isn't a stone to place directly into planters or gardens as it damaged by sunshine and water, Fuchsite adds a dose of fairy magic to nature-themed adventuring, whether you're out wilderness camping or simply shopping for houseplants at your local garden shop. Very helpful for connecting to plant-based health and healing, keep Fuchsite nearby as you research holistic healing for help zoning in on what is best for *your* unique body and well-being. If Fuchsite's energy feels slightly ungrounded or 'flaky' to you, try *Ruby in Fuchsite*, its grounded cousin, as an alternative.

NOTES Fuchsite's distinctive sparkle comes from being a variety of mica, a flaky mineral that creates the shimmer in cosmetics. Fuchsite is most commonly sold as small, raw pieces that leave a fun sparkle on whatever they touch. It is often found embedded with little rubies, creating the beautiful combination Ruby in Fuchsite. Pronounced *fook-site*, also commonly called Green Muscovite.

ALMANDINE

Garnet

PASSION + SENSUALITY + CREATIVITY + GROUNDING

Colour Wine red to almost black

Born in China, USA, Mexico

Chakras Root, Sacral

Water Cleansing ☒ Y ☐ N

MAGIC Like juice-stained lips on a hot summer night, cherry-coloured Almandine Garnets are stones of sensuality and earthiness. This crystal is all about generating passion: passionate creativity, passionate sensuality, passionate living. As it's important to have the grounding of a 'safe space' in order to bravely explore unknown ideas and unchartered passions, Garnet makes an ideal adventure partner as it helps you keep boundaries firmly established and respected while also removing inhibitions and blockages. An important ally in times of crisis, it's no coincidence that Garnet jewellery reached the height of popularity after both World Wars, as it helps heal and regenerate from trauma and chaos. Almandine Garnet can also activate grounded *kundalini* energy (a mystical energy connected to creativity and spiritual enlightenment), and is excellent for regulating sex drives and enhancing sensual explorations – try tucking one under your mattress to spice up your love life. Great for manifesting, don't forget to get Garnet out on new moon nights to charge up your dreams and desires!

NOTES Garnets occur in a vast variety of colours, with Almandine Garnet being the most abundant and affordable variety. Although most commonly sold as small tumbled stones, Almandine Garnet naturally forms as round, faceted crystals that are worth searching out as they have a unique, raw potency. Garnet is both a traditional and Ayurverdic birthstone for January.

PINK

Halite

CLARITY + DETOX + ENERGY PURIFIER

✳ **Colour** Light pink
◉ **Born in** California, Poland
🜨 **Chakra** Heart
◇ **Water Cleansing** ☐ Y ☒ N

MAGIC A salt crystal, Halite is a purifier
of energies and environments. Formed
from the salt of evaporated ancient seas,
its delicate pink colour is caused by tiny
sea creatures – I'm not joking, take a whiff
and smell for yourself! Salty Pink Halite
works hard to help 'evaporate' emotional
traumas, heartbreak and sadness, and can
bring fresh clarity to situations of the heart.
Do you have a hunch that the relationship
you're in isn't so healthy? Do some of your
friends or family always leave you feeling
more drained than supported? Are you
an emotional empath *aka* are you affected

emotionally by other people's 'stuff' in a
way that destabilises you? Halite will help
you separate from toxic or non-nourishing
situations and people by clearing out
whatever and whomever needs to leave your
life, and disconnecting you from whatever
isn't yours to deal with. A great crystal
for bedrooms, Halite will stay hard at work
cleansing and clearing while you snooze.

NOTES Halite is a sodium mineral better
known as plain old 'rock salt', mined
worldwide for a huge variety of industrial
purposes including melting icy winter roads.
It forms in many colours, with lovely cubic
specimens most common in the colours pink,
white, and (more rarely) blue. Halite 'melts'
in wet environments, so be sure to keep
clusters very dry, this is not a crystal for
humid bathrooms.

Hematite

BALANCING + RECHARGE + GROUNDING + PROTECTION

✳ **Colour** Dark grey with a metallic sheen

⌖ **Born in** Brazil, USA, China

♋ **Chakra** Root

💧 **Water Cleansing** ☒ Y ☐ N
Polished pieces only

MAGIC We are each encased in our own personal magnetic sphere, similar to the magnetic field encompassing our planet. Hematite, an iron-based mineral with magnetic properties, is an extremely powerful crystal tool for recharging your personal wiring and energy grid. Do you get lost in unproductive daydreaming? Hematite will help anchor you in the present moment, and is the perfect stone for those who tend to get stuck in the past or future. It is a vital stone for rebalancing, especially when life's stressors bring you close to short-circuiting. Slip a small polished Hematite into your pocket to recharge and rebalance during your daily activities, or tuck a piece into your chair for continuous grounding during your workday. Adding Hematite to your bath (by your feet) will help you recentre and relax at the end of a long day. Hematite can also help you mine down into issues buried deep in your emotional psyche, history, and ancestral lineage. This crystal doesn't mess around, so if Hematite feels too intense (you'll know – it just won't feel right), try Black Tourmaline or Smoky Quartz instead, as they ground and recharge in a gentler manner than Hematite.

NOTES Raw Hematite is often a dusty dark red colour, and morphs into its recognisable grey metallic sheen once polished. Hematite becomes magnetic when heated, however most crystal healers prefer working with natural (unheated) specimens. Hematite is a very dense mineral, and its weightiness is a distinctive identifying feature among darkly coloured polished stones.

Iceland Spar

CLARITY + PERSPECTIVE + FOCUS + INSPIRATION

✳ **Colour** Crystal clear

⌖ **Born in** Mexico, Morocco

❧ **Chakras** 3rd Eye, Crown

◌ **Water Cleansing** ☐ Y ☒ N

MAGIC *Sometimes all you really need is a new way of looking at something.* New perspectives offer fresh clarity and inspiration. Luckily for us, crystal-clear Iceland Spar is here to help. This geometric crystal naturally forms in perfect rhomboid shapes, rainbow-filled parallelograms that provide a new filter through which to see the world. Lie with this crystal on your third eye when you are having a hard time choosing between options or making an important decision. Hold a crystal up to your eye and gaze through to give your subconscious a shift in perspective. Iceland Spar offers the invaluable gift of reminding us that this world is nothing more (and nothing less) than an optical illusion. Nothing is permanent, nothing is insurmountable, and nothing – absolutely nothing – is impossible!

NOTES Iceland Spar is a variety of Calcite, unique for its clarity and double refraction abilities. The term 'cleavage' refers to a mineral's ability to break along a flat line, and if you ever happen to drop this crystal you'll get to see that in action, as it can only break along a straight line. Iceland Spar was originally discovered in Iceland, but today's specimens usually come from Mexico and Morocco. A softer mineral whose sharp edges can chip easily, take care in how you use and store it. Also known as Clear or Optical Calcite.

Jade

INTUITION + LUCK + PROSPERITY + SUCCESS

⊛ **Colour** Shades of green
⚱ **Born in** China, Myanmar, Africa
⬡ **Chakra** Solar Plexus
◊ **Water Cleansing** ☒ Y ☐ N

MAGIC Jade is a classic stone of abundance and wealth, prized by everyone from the ancient Aztecs to modern tech moguls. The green stone we call 'Jade' is actually two minerals with very different histories, Jadeite and Nephrite. The name Jade was bestowed by conquistadors on the green Jadeite rocks they saw native Aztecs and Mayans using for medicinal purposes, while Nephrite has been treasured by the Chinese for millennia as a stone of spiritual purity and intellectual clarity. For modern crystal lovers, Jade remains a classic choice for abundance, wealth and good fortune. Jade is a crystal for *getting to know yourself*, an important factor behind its legacy of luck and success. Because when you know yourself – when you get really clear and honest about who you are and why you came here – you can't help but focus your time and energy on things that are in natural alignment with your gifts and skills. Which leads to (you guessed it) success and 'luck' in the material world, as well as a deep, fulfilling sense of prosperity.

NOTES Jadeite and Nephrite form in many colours, bright green Jadeite being the most valuable variety. Most tumbled 'Jade' stones aren't actually Jadeite or Nephrite, as a wide selection of green-coloured minerals are sold as various varieties of 'Jade.' Although not authentic Jade, these stones still offer valuable metaphysical gifts.

Jasper

PHYSICAL/EMOTIONAL STRENGTH + GROUNDING + STABILISING

✳ **Colour** All shades of the rainbow

◎ **Born in** Worldwide

☁ **Chakra** Root + varies by colour

◇ **Water Cleansing** ☒ Y ☐ N

MAGIC *Solid As A Rock*. Jaspers are extremely 'solid' crystals, no-nonsense stones that hold an uncomplicated, stable energy. A mineral family of densely-packed quartz micro-crystals, Jaspers are grounding rocks that can help you gain strength in both your physical body and emotions. This is a great crystal for 'earthing', the healthy practice of grounding into the earth's energy: hold a Jasper crystal while you sit outside with your bare feet touching the ground for a healing zap of Vitamin G, aka *grounding*. A crystal chakra layout using only Jasper crystals is like a visit to the chiropractor, extremely stabilising and aligning. Forming in all colours of the rainbow, all Jaspers have root chakra energy as their base, with aspects of other chakras according to their colour. *Red Jasper* is historically the most popular variety, famed since antiquity for its health-giving and protective magic, and the two varieties pictured are personal favourites: *Green Kambaba Jasper* roots you into peaceful nature energies, and *Ocean Jasper*, a multicoloured variety, is a gorgeous stone of flow and grace.

NOTES These strong, durable stones are an opaque variety of the mineral Chalcedony. Found worldwide in 'massive' (non-crystallized) form, Jasper is broken down into smaller pieces and polished for sale as a variety of tumbled stones and polished specimens.

BLUE

Kyanite

ENERGY PURIFIER + CLEANSING + COMMUNICATION

✳ **Colour** Pearly blue
◎ **Born in** Brazil
🜨 **Chakra** Throat
◌ **Water Cleansing** ☒ Y ☐ N

MAGIC Blue Kyanite cleanses and opens your throat chakra, cutting through communication fears and blockages to help you bravely share your truth from an ego-less, honest place. Forming in unique, striated crystal 'blades', Kyanite works like an energy antenna, flowing negative energy out and away from your body and aura while also filtering positive energy back into your personal space. Keep a piece in your pocket or tucked in your clothing when going into a challenging meeting or difficult conversation for support, clarity, and general kickassery. I keep a little bowl of these beautiful blue stones near my computer for help working through my inbox with efficiency and inspiration. An energy-filtering crystal, Kyanite can help clear the air after arguments or emotional conversations: hold one up to your throat for adrenal rebalancing, and wave a crystal in each corner of the room to purify any lingering heavy vibes. For extra-strength cleansing, use in combination with a ritual smoke cleanse, such as palo santo or sage. According to Melody, pioneering author of the modern crystal revival, Kyanite is self-cleansing and never requires energy cleansing or clearing.

NOTES Kyanite comes in many colours, each with its own unique metaphysical qualities. Blue Kyanite is the most common variety, followed by Black Kyanite, a grounding crystal. Thin Kyanite blades can easily break, so use with care; polished pieces are much more durable. Kyanite commonly forms embedded in white Quartz.

Labradorite

BE HERE NOW + INTUITION + WISDOM + PROTECTION

⊛ **Colour** Grey-green with multicoloured iridescence

◎ **Born in** Madagascar, Finland

❀ **Chakra** 3rd Eye

◊ **Water Cleansing** ☒ Y ☐ N

MAGIC All shades of the human eye can be seen in Labradorite's mystical, multicoloured flash: green, blue, hazel and black. A stone of many eyes, I call Labradorite the 'Stone of Seeing', as this is a crystal for perceiving what is real and true in the present moment. Labradorite releases you from things that you are ready to move on from, everything from toxic friendships to bad habits hanging on from past lives. *Be Here Now*. Intuition is a form of seeing, and Labradorite is one of the best stones for enhancing your connection with intuition; meditate with Labradorite on your third eye to see below the surface of situations, relationships and reality itself. Keep Labradorite close to gain access to insights and wisdoms that lie just below the obvious, and to help you see things in a new light. Sleeping with a piece under your pillow or bed is a great way to absorb this crystal's gifts. A protective stone, Labradorite strengthens your aura, deflecting and protecting you from any less-than-bright energies.

NOTES Originally discovered in Labrador, Canada, modern specimens mainly come from Madagascar. *Spectrolite* is a rarer form of Labradorite traditionally found only in Finland, unique for its bright orange, yellow, and fuschia flash. Labradorite forms in opaque chunky masses, and though unpolished specimens do have a raw beauty, this beautiful mineral's colour and iridescence is best seen once polished.

Lapis Lazuli

TRANSFORMATION + HONESTY
+ SELF-AWARENESS + MYSTICISM

- **Colour** Blue with flecks of white + gold
- **Born in** Afghanistan, Pakistan
- **Chakras** 3rd Eye, Throat
- **Care** May be too intense for bedrooms
- **Water Cleansing** ☐ Y ☒ N

MAGIC Regal Lapis Lazuli has been treasured by royalty, priests, and holy healers for thousands of years, adorning countless precious objects with its mysterious blue hue. A favourite of the Ancient Egyptians, who considered Lapis Lazuli to contain immortal powers, this stone is all about stories, histories, and authenticity. We each have our 'story', our own version of history which we cling to and identify with, both positively and negatively. Lapis Lazuli forces you to put down the security blanket of your stories. It asks you to do the hard work of transcending, reminding you that the past *doesn't actually exist*, and empowers you to take responsibility for your own choices. It also helps you integrate wisdom learned from past experiences, past lives, and the lessons that come to you through the legacy of your ancestors. If this sounds like a lot, it is. This stone requires action, so it's generally better for altars than bedrooms, and many find it too intense to wear as everyday jewellery. Lapis Lazuli will help you get real, honest, and authentic. *Lapis Lazuli = Stop Making Excuses*.

NOTES Genuine Lapis Lazuli has an unmistakeable deep blue saturation, and often shimmers with flecks of golden Pyrite. Lighter-blue Sodalite and dyed Howlite are often passed off as Lapis Lazuli, but these generally have more white colouration in them as well as an absence of Pyrite.

Lepidolite

CALMING + STABILISING + LIFTS DEPRESSION AND ANXIETY

Colour Silvery lilac or rose
Born in Brazil
Chakras Heart, Crown, 3rd Eye
Water Cleansing ☒ Y ☐ N
Polished pieces only

MAGIC *Balance*. Something we all need, vital for functioning as a healthy human. And something we lose touch with all too easily. Fortunately for us, silvery Lepidolite sparkles to our emotional rescue! This shimmering mica crystal is stuffed full of Lithium – the same mineral used in powerful psychiatric pharmaceuticals – and is one of the best calming and stabilising crystals for whenever life gets overwhelming. A natural antidepressant, this is a stone to keep very close when stress, anxiety or depression gets the upper hand. From colicky babies to overwhelmed teens, and from sleep-deprived new mothers to sensitive artistic souls, absolutely everyone can benefit from Lepidolite's soothing magic. Because everyone has times when they desperately need to be reminded that everything is okay, that everything will be okay, and that you – beautiful, wonderful you – are more than okay, you are perfect. ***And you are doing your best***. A wise man once wrote, 'Be kind, for everyone you meet is fighting a great battle', Let Lepidolite help you cope with life's daily battles and challenges so that you can shine ever more brightly, blissfully and peacefully.

NOTES Lepidolite forms in a wide variety of raw shapes, including flat slabs that easily peel into very thin layers, and glittering, scaly clusters ribboned with white Quartz. Lepidolite does form in colours other than lilac and rose, but specimens are much less common. Clusters with bits of Pink Tourmaline mixed in have a lovely, heart-opening energy.

Malachite

COMMITMENT + SELF-WORTH + WILLPOWER + FORGIVENESS

✳ **Colour** Swirling green stripes

◎ **Born in** The Congo, Namibia, Mexico

☯ **Chakras** Heart, Solar Plexus

◇ **Water Cleansing** ☒ Y ☐ N
Polished pieces only

MAGIC Swirling green Malachite holds powerful heart energies. The activated yang to Rose Quartz's gentle yin, this ancient heart stone is a supportive gift for the special men in your life, as well as anyone who needs help with willpower and forgiveness (and let's be honest, who doesn't?). Holding an unusual combo of heart and solar plexus chakra energies, meditate or nap with Malachite placed on either chakra point to work through blockages related to self-worth. This stone strengthens your ability to stay true to commitments, both promises you've made to others, and the essential commitment of showing kindness and forgiveness to yourself. A powerful ally for those struggling with issues related to infidelity, honesty, and addictions, Malachite is that no-nonsense friend everyone needs, the one who actually calls you out on the negative patterns you keep repeating and helps you get honest about your issues of self-worth and willpower. Malachite helps you stop holding yourself back from being the very best, most honest, and most real version of YOU possible.

NOTES As Malachite is a copper-based mineral it can be toxic if ingested; keep away from little mouths and do not use in drinkable elixirs. Most commonly sold as tumbled, polished and carved pieces, it also forms as bristly specimens sold under the names Fibrous, Velvet, or Silky Malachite.

RAINBOW

Moonstone

INTUITION + EMPOWERED FEMININITY + MOON MAGIC

✳ **Colour** Milky-white with a blue flash
◉ **Born in** India
⚬ **Chakras** 3rd Eye, Crown
◇ **Water Cleansing** ☒ Y ☐ N

MAGIC Like the moon shimmering in the night sky, full of mysterious majesty, Rainbow Moonstone connects us with the mysteries of life, those deeper truths that lie just on the edge of reality. Moonstone gently welcomes you to step into your subconscious and inner knowing; meditate with this stone on your third eye for cosmic intuitions and inspirations. A stone of the Divine Feminine, Moonstone swirls with the magic of wise old women, fertile mothers, ethereal goddesses and mystical mermaids. Like the moon herself, Moonstone is deeply connected with the push and pull of feminine cycles, and is a soothing companion for when emotions and hormones are heightened. This stone awakens radiant and empowered femininity, and will help unleash the goddess energy that flows deep within each of us (and Moonstone most certainly isn't only for those with female bodies, everyone can benefit from its powerful gifts of intuition and life-giving sensuality!). A powerful moon-magic stone, don't forget to bring your Moonstones out on new and full moon nights for extra-potent manifesting.

NOTES Rainbow Moonstone is the flashiest of Moonstone varieties with its beautiful blue shine, called 'labradorescence' (technically, Rainbow Moonstone is a form of the mineral Labradorite). A favourite gemstone since ancient times, Moonstone is widely available as polished pieces and tumbled stones. It often forms with black Granite, creating a beautiful black and white combo within one specimen. Moonstone is a traditional birthstone for June, and a zodiac birthstone for Cancer.

BLACK

Obsidian

PROTECTION + ENERGY-SHIELDING + DECISIONS + GRIEF

⚘ **Colour** Glossy jet-black
◷ **Born in** USA
◈ **Chakra** Root
◌ **Water Cleansing** ☒ Y ☐ N

MAGIC Formed by powerful volcanic eruptions, glossy Black Obsidian is a stone of protection and divination. A natural 'glass' created from rapidly cooled lava, Obsidian is not technically a mineral as it formed too quickly to create an internal crystalline structure. This gives Black Obsidian an unusual vibration, unique within the mineral kingdom. Obsidian's #1 gift is energy deflection – it wraps an impenetrable shield around you, making it a valuable stone for sensitive souls and emotional empaths. Holding a piece in your hand, imagine a jet-black shield rising up between you and the source of your worry or fear. Use this magic wisely, however. An Obsidian shield is useful for protection in circumstances that can overwhelm your nervous system, such as large crowds. But this isn't the crystal to take with you to social gatherings, as it will shield your energy from connecting with others, very likely making you feel invisible. Also a crystal of *divination* (the mystical art of seeing the future), Obsidian is useful when you need help making difficult decisions: hold a crystal in your hand, quiet your thoughts, and observe what materialises in your inner mind. You'll know what to do.

NOTES Black Obsidian is a hard and brittle material, generally available only in small raw or polished pieces. Rough-edged raw pieces (pictured) are my preference from an energetic standpoint. *Apache Tears*, a rounded variety of Obsidian found in the American Southwest, are some of the very best stones for processing grief and loss.

Pyrite

CONFIDENCE + LUCK + ABUNDANCE + PRODUCTIVITY + CREATIVITY

✳ **Colour** Metallic gold
◉ **Born in** Peru, Spain, China
⟆ **Chakras** Solar Plexus
♡ **Care** May be too intense for bedrooms
◊ **Water Cleansing** ☐ Y ☒ N

MAGIC *Rock On, Magic Maker*. A crystal of supercharged creativity and Get-It-Done productivity, golden Pyrite is a powerhouse of confidence, action and abundance. Given its fiery name by the Ancient Greeks upon discovering that striking Pyrite against steel causes sparks to fly (*pyr* = 'fire' in Greek), this metallic mineral continues to spark major magic for modern crystal lovers. Keep a cluster near and don't say I didn't tell you as dream collaborations, creative inspirations, and lucky breaks manifest with unstoppable abundance! A solar plexus crystal, Pyrite lights a fire in your belly to help burn through procrastination and self-doubt, giving you the courage to share your gifts with the world. Meditate with Pyrite to boost self-esteem, confidence, and creative inspiration. One of my Essential Rockstars, Pyrite is best kept in spaces where you wish to feel active and inspired, and is an ideal workspace crystal. Stash in handbags, wallets and cash registers for manifesting abundance and $$$. Although Pyrite may have fairly earned its nickname of 'Fool's Gold' for tricking countless treasure hunters into thinking they'd struck gold, you would be the fool to miss out on adding this crystal's golden abundance to your life!

NOTES Pyrite commonly forms as completely metallic clusters of small, geometric crystals. Spanish Pyrite is unique for its perfect golden squares (pictured). Pyrite dulls and rusts when exposed to moisture, so don't leave it outside overnight after moon rituals. Clusters with Clear Quartz inclusions are extra-strong doses of Pyrite power.

CLEAR

Quartz

TRANSFORMATION + CLARITY + HEALING

⊛ **Colour** Crystal clear

🆑 **Born in** Worldwide

☯ **Chakras** All

◌ **Water Cleansing** ☒ Y ☐ N

MAGIC Revered as a powerful tool of transformative magic since time began, Clear Quartz lightens up, brightens up, and powers up our lives with its rainbow rays of magic. It's no exaggeration to say that Clear Quartz quite literally runs our modern world: clocks wouldn't work without the tiny pieces of Quartz that keep them precisely ticking, our beloved techie toys wouldn't exist without Quartz's electricity-conducting skills... *very simply, this is an essential crystal for everywhere and everyone*. A natural prism holding the full, sparkling spectrum of a rainbow, Clear Quartz crystals are master healers, energy transmitters, and connectors to higher consciousness. Easily programmable as a personal magic tool, simply concentrate on your desired energy, action, outcome or feeling while holding your crystal, and *voilà*: a powerful, tireless guide and cheerleader in crystal form. One of my Essential Rockstars, Clear Quartz amplifies the effects of all other crystals and can clear them of stagnant energy. Follow your intuition when deciding how and where to use Clear Quartz, as this crystal will most definitely guide you. *Clear Quartz = a crystal for serious Levelling Up!*

NOTES The most abundant crystal on our planet, Quartz is found all over the world, although most specimens currently on the market come from Arkansas (USA) and Brazil. Quartz crystals can be easily identified from other minerals by their six-sided crystal points.

Rhodonite

LETTING GO + HEARTBREAK
+ STABILISING + BOUNDARIES

Colour Swirls of pink + black + white
Born in Madagascar, Australia, USA
Chakras Heart, Root
Water Cleansing ☒ Y ☐ N

MAGIC First discovered in the late 1700s in the Urals, a mystical Russian mountain range, Rhodonite was given the name 'Eagle Stone' by locals upon witnessing the phenomenon of eagles carrying small pieces of Rhodonite back to their nests. Eagles are animal totems of courage, wisdom and strength, and Rhodonite holds a similar fiercely protective, boundary-strengthening vibration. This pink-swirled stone is a crystal for deep heart healing and grief releasing. A stabilising tonic for heartbreak, Rhodonite is a valuable crystal ally for difficult transitions of all kinds, from relationships or career changes, to illness and death. Lay a stone on your heart chakra, breathe deeply, and allow the cracks in your heart to be filled with healing and light.

A stone of compassion, Rhodonite releases stuck, fearful energies related to self-worth and self-love, and helps you establish healthy boundaries. A powerful crystal to use for self-healing rituals including baths, meditation and massage.

NOTES Rhodonite is almost always found in massive form, and sold as polished pieces. Pink-red Rhodonite crystal clusters do form but they are rare and expensive. Rhodonite's cousin with whom it's often confused, *Rhodochrosite*, has similar pink and white swirls, but Rhodonite can be identified by its inclusion of black manganese dioxide. Officially named only in 1819, Rhodonite is the official state gem of Massachusetts (USA) and considered by many to be the national stone of Russia, although never officially titled. While Russia is a historical source of Rhodonite, modern specimens are sourced elsewhere due to availability.

Rose Quartz

LOVE + COMPASSION + KINDNESS + TENDERNESS

✳ **Colour** Rosy pink
◎ **Born in** Madagascar
♋ **Chakra** Heart
♡ **Care** Fades in direct sunlight
◊ **Water Cleansing** ☒ Y ☐ N

MAGIC The classic Love Crystal, Rose Quartz is legendary for its ability to heal heartbreak, attract new love, and open hearts to new levels of forgiveness, compassion, and Love, Love, Love. Don't be fooled into thinking this crystal is a lightweight by its candy-pink hue, as Rose Quartz is one of the most nurturing crystals in the crystal kingdom. All of life's many forms of love – romantic, family, self-love, Universal – are strengthened by powerful Rose Quartz. The crystal of Venus, goddess of love and beauty, try adding Rose Quartz pieces to your bath to transform bathing into a love-filled, healing ritual. When feeling emotionally low, place a Rose Quartz on your chest and visualise a gentle pink light filling your heart space, lifting all heaviness away. One of my Essential Rockstars, I've yet to encounter a person who couldn't benefit from adding some Rose Quartz magic into their life. This is a wonderful crystal to keep in any and all rooms of the house – *the more Rose Quartz in your life, the Lovelier!*

NOTES Rose Quartz is almost always found as large specimens with no crystal edges, which are broken down into a huge variety of raw and polished shapes. Rose Quartz as crystallised clusters are very rare, expensive and small, so if you see one sold relatively cheaply it's most likely dyed Quartz or Calcite – pretty, but not actually Rose Quartz!

GOLDEN

Rutilated Quartz

ANGELIC GUIDANCE + OPTIMISM + ENERGY ZAPS

✳ **Colour** Clear with internal golden fibres
♂ **Born in** Brazil
✿ **Chakras** Solar Plexus, Crown
◌ **Water Cleansing** ☒ Y ☐ N

MAGIC Filled with shimmering golden strands of titanium, Rutilated Quartz holds a vibration of hope-filled optimism and positivity. Just like the fairytale moral of Rapunzel, that golden-haired damsel in distress, this happy mineral helps remind us to *never give up hope*, no matter how dark or difficult our current circumstances. If you're struggling with depression or a general lack of energy, Rutilated Quartz is a great crystal for giving yourself uplifting energy 'zaps': place a crystal on your solar plexus chakra and let it work its antidepressive, energising magic. It's also great for making energising water elixirs. Keep Rutilated Quartz close whenever you feel completely overwhelmed, as this golden-flecked crystal connects you with angelic assistance. For a supercharged infusion of celestial support, place eight crystals in a circle around your body and lie quietly, breathing deeply, for at least ten minutes. I guarantee that you'll be flying high on golden wings by the time you finish your meditation!

NOTES Rutilated Quartz forms when Clear Quartz encases already existing hairlike strands of Rutile crystals. Commonly available both as polished stones and natural crystal points, Rutilated Quartz also forms with black and/or red Rutile inclusions, which have a different energy than the golden variety. Natural underground radiation can darken specimens to create *Rutilated Smoky Quartz*, a less common variety. Also called Rutile Quartz, historic names include Venus Hairstone, Cupid's Darts and Flèches d'Amour (Love Arrows).

Selenite

CLEANSING + CLEARING + MOON MAGIC

✳ **Colour** Clear to opaque white
⊘ **Born in** Mexico, Morocco, USA
⬥ **Chakras** Crown, 3rd Eye
◊ **Water Cleansing** ☐ Y ☒ N

MAGIC Named after Selene, mythical goddess of the moon, Selenite is a no-fuss crystal famed for its powerful and wide-ranging cleansing abilities. This is the ultimate crystal for easily cleansing and clearing energies and auras. Try keeping a piece of Selenite near your front door for a quick energy rinse when you return home at the end of a long day: simply wave Selenite over and around the edges of your body (don't forget your back!), and it will wipe you clear from any sticky vibes or energies that might have latched onto you. There are a myriad of ways to use Selenite's purifying magic: a larger piece kept near computers, televisions and routers is helpful for balancing disruptive electrical discharge; store a piece in your fridge and kitchen cupboards to keep food fresh; and keep Selenite in bedrooms to calm restless sleepers and ward off any nightmares. A classic and very effective option for cleansing stagnant energy from other crystals, lay your crystals on a piece of Selenite for at least 4 hours to cleanse and clear them. And of course, don't forget to add this moonlight crystal to your new and full moon rituals for potent, high-vibe manifesting and energy cleansing!

NOTES Selenite is a soft form of the mineral Gypsum and scratches and flakes easily, so use with care. It is widely available in an affordable variety of shapes and sizes. Flat pieces for using to cleanse other crystals are often sold as Selenite plates or wands.

Shungite

DETOX + PURIFY + PROTECTION

Colour Metallic black
Born in Russia
Chakra Root
Care May be too intense for bedrooms
Water Cleansing ☒ Y ☐ N

MAGIC Shungite is primordial-level magic, a carbon rock formed billions of years ago from ancient algae. Shungite has quite a reputation as a health cure-all, especially when used in water elixirs as a purifier, however, it's important to be aware that Shungite is available in two distinct varieties which should be used differently. *Black Shungite* (pictured, also called Classic Shungite) has a dull black sheen and is the more common, less expensive variety. Generally ground up and re-formed into polished shapes such as tumbled stones, beads, and pyramids, this form of Shungite contains only 30–35% carbon and should **not** be used for water purification and elixirs, as other minerals in it may be toxic. Use Black Shungite for protection grids, rituals and meditations, and place around your home and electronics for energy neutralisation and protection. Rarer, more expensive *Silver Shungite* (also called Noble or Elite Shungite) has a metallic sheen and is only available in raw pieces as it isn't durable enough to be polished. Made mostly of pure carbon, Silver Shungite is the only type to use for water purification. Believed to cleanse water from all impurities, place a piece in a jug of water, steep for at least a few hours, and drink to your health!

NOTES Shungite is technically a rock, rather than a mineral or crystal, as it is made from organic material. It is found almost exclusively in one area of the world, near the Russian village of Shunga.

Smoky Quartz

ENERGY CLEANSING + STRESS RELIEF
+ GROUNDING + MEDITATION

✳ **Colour** Translucent to opaque brown

◉ **Born in** Worldwide

⟠ **Chakra** Root

♡ **Care** Fades in direct sunlight

◌ **Water Cleansing** ☒ Y ☐ N

MAGIC Smoky Quartz is one of the most powerful crystal tools for energy transmutation. It holds a similar cleansing magic as its cousin Amethyst, but where Amethyst goes high, Smoky Quartz goes deep: this dark crystal swiftly moves negative energies out of your aura, carrying them deep into the earth for grounding and transmutation. Smoky Quartz makes a phenomenal meditation partner as it is simultaneously stabilising and consciousness-expanding. Follow your intuition as you experiment with adding one to your meditation practice; popular uses include placing a crystal at the base of the spine (between inner thighs or on the tail bone), or placing a crystal touching the sole of each foot. If you don't have a meditation practice, just taking a nap with this crystal in bed with you will work rejuvenating miracles. Had a stress-filled day? Try a *Smoky Soak*: place a crystal point on each corner of your bathtub, the points facing in towards you, to recentre and melt away stress. Pop some Rose Quartz into your bathwater for an extra dose of magic and *aaahhh*: instant relaxation and deep healing. Keep this energy powerhouse wherever you feel its smoky magic is needed.

NOTES Clear or lightly smoky quartz crystals are sometimes exposed to radiation to darken them. These irradiated, 'treated' specimens can often be identified by their opaque black colouring. Smoky Quartz is commonly available in a vast variety of tumbled and polished shapes, as well as natural clusters and crystal points.

Spirit Quartz

JOY + INSPIRATION + GENEROSITY + COMMUNITY

✳ **Colour** Shades of lavender, yellow, white

☌ **Born in** South Africa

☍ **Chakras** Crown, 3rd Eye

♡ **Care** Fades in direct sunlight

◇ **Water Cleansing** ☒ Y ☐ N

MAGIC *Crystallized Joy*. Sweet, uplifting Spirit Quartz sends a powerful vibration of joy out through every one of its many crystal points, creating sparkling energy fireworks within the entire space surrounding it. A crystal of transcendence, Spirit Quartz reminds you to always radiate your magnificent energies *outwards* into the world, purifying any tendencies towards self-absorption. Helping you get unstuck from ego, it enhances your ability to be compassionate and generous. Spirit Quartz is very supportive for anyone whose work includes channelling healing and transformative energy for others, and

is an ideal crystal for healers, teachers, and creatives. Spirit Quartz is a favourite to use at the crown chakra during crystal healings, and a little point carried in a pocket or bag is perfect for keeping this crystal's magic with you while out and about. One of my Essential Rockstars, radiant Spirit Quartz is one of my most uplifting crystals in the crystal kingdom, and will spread inspiration, healing and sparkles of joy wherever it is kept.

NOTES Spirit Quartz is a variety of Amethyst, and is easily identified by its unique formation of multiple tiny points around a larger point. Cactus Quartz is an alternate name, and single points covered with tiny crystals are sometimes called Fairy Quartz. Because Spirit Quartz is found only in one small area of South Africa, quality specimens continue to become rarer and more expensive.

Sulphur

IMMUNE-BOOSTING + HAPPINESS + CREATIVITY

✵ **Colour** Neon yellow
◎ **Born in** Bolivia, Italy
❀ **Chakra** Solar Plexus
♡ **Care** Cracks in direct sunlight
◊ **Water Cleansing** ☐ Y ☒ N

MAGIC Ever wondered what the biblical phrase 'fire and brimstone' referred to? Well you're in luck, my friend, wonder no more: this gorgeous, neon crystal is real-life brimstone. Born from ancient volcanic activity, crystallised Sulphur is a fantastic helper for detoxifying, purifying, and uplifting. Are you a 'glass-half-empty' type of person? Bring a piece of this sunshine stone into your life and let it work its sunny magic to transform your mood and uplift your outlook. Holding a joyfully fizzy energy, Sulphur's neon vibes help remind you how to live with a sense of child-like wonder. This is a perfect crystal for spaces where you get creative, whether that's a corporate cubicle or artist atelier. Great for increasing immune system vitality and strength, Sulphur's energy feels like a happy giggle encapsulated in a crystal; place it on your solar plexus whenever you need a bubbly boost of sunshine. And no, you're not imagining things, Sulphur crystals do have a faint – but unmistakeable – eggy odour!

NOTES A pure element (S), Sulphur crystals can crumble easily, so handle with care. Sulphur is mined worldwide for a variety of industrial uses, with beautiful crystallised specimens historically found near Italian volcanoes. Modern specimens mainly come from Bolivia, and form in combination with a white mineral matrix. While Sulphur is not toxic, specimens may contain traces of minerals that are (e.g. cinnabar), so wash your hands after handling and keep away from children and pets. Sulfur is an alternative spelling.

Tangerine Quartz

SEXUAL HEALING + BODY ISSUES + SHAME RELEASE + SENSUALITY

✳ **Colour** Pale orange to deep rust
◈ **Born in** Brazil, Madagascar
❀ **Chakra** Sacral
◊ **Water Cleansing** ☒ Y ☐ N

MAGIC *Sexual Healing*. We all have things to heal related to sexuality and body image. Even if you're the unicorn among us who has had only 100% uplifting, body-affirming, and consensual sexual experiences (anyone out there raising their hand?), there are stories of shame and transgressions running deep through each of our bloodlines and ancestral history. Tangerine Quartz is a beautiful stone for liquidating and transforming stored shame, pain, and negative body associations and experiences. Place one of these dusky orange crystals on your lower stomach or between your inner thighs, breathe deeply, and imagine

a warm orange glow permeating your lower body, relaxing and melting your hips, lower back, and sexual organs. If you feel the need for extra grounding, place Smoky Quartz or Black Tourmaline crystals at the bottom of your feet. Since Tangerine Quartz activates stagnant energy in your sacral chakra, this is also a fantastic crystal for lighting juicy fires in the bedroom: put a small point of the crystal under your mattress and let it work its magic!

NOTES Tangerine Quartz is Clear Quartz with a natural micro-coating of iron hematite on either the surface or interior of each crystal. As polishing would remove the orange colouring in many cases, these crystals have a dull orange finish and almost always have some chipped edges. Natural small points are the easiest to find; larger clusters are less common and can be expensive.

GOLDEN

Tiger's Eye

SOCIAL CHANGE + ACTIVATING + COURAGE + PROTECTION

✳ **Colour** Iridescent brown + gold stripes
◉ **Born in** South Africa, Australia, Brazil
�ึ **Chakras** Sacral, Solar Plexus, Root
♡ **Care** May be too intense for bedrooms
◊ **Water Cleansing** ☒ Y ☐ N

MAGIC I've polled my crystal-loving pals and we all agree: Tiger's Eye brings to mind the shag carpets, muted photo filters, and bellbottom jeans of a very specific era. This stone really rocks those retro '70s vibes, and not just because it was a popular gemstone. Tiger's Eye holds a strongly 'activating' energy, similar to the spirit of that volatile decade of intense social change. This stone can feel uncomfortable to many people as it pokes tucked-away corners of psyches, bringing up itchy, unpleasant feelings and pushing boundaries. I recommend using Tiger's Eye in combination with an energy-moving stone such as Amethyst, to help transmute the energetic 'sludge' this crystal can loosen up. Lay both crystals together on the chakra you would like to stimulate. Tiger's Eye also has a long history of being used as a protection talisman. Although a favourite with children and men, Tiger's Eye tends to inspire a love-hate relationship in many women. If you feel put off by its vibration, try seeking out a non-polished piece, as the energies of raw Tiger's Eye flow differently and feel more organic and approachable to many women.

NOTES Tiger's Eye is a variety of quartz filled with inclusions of (non-harmful!) asbestos fibres, creating its golden-brown shimmer. The iridescence created by these fibres creates luminescent bands visible under certain lighting, similar to a cat's eye. Forming in several colours, the most common variety is a golden-brown colour, followed by blue and red variations.

BLACK

Tourmaline

PROTECTION + GROUNDING + RECHARGING

❋ **Colour** Opaque jet-black
◔ **Born in** Brazil
☬ **Chakra** Root
◊ **Water Cleansing** ☒ Y ☐ N

MAGIC Black Tourmaline = *Crystal Bodyguard Extraordinaire*. An energy heavyweight, this crystal is a must-have for its ability to keep you anchored in this physical reality. Vitally important for balancing the heady vibes generated by other crystals, keep one nearby for continuous grounding and recharging, and sleep with a crystal at your feet whenever you feel untethered or unsafe. As an energy protector Black Tourmaline is unparalleled; think of this stone as a guard dog who tirelessly protects your personal boundaries and deflects negative energy. Place a crystal near the entrance to your home, office, dorm room, etc. to keep all dark forces out. Tuck a small piece into your clothing, pocket or wallet for on-the-go protection, and don't forget to stash one in your car to keep you safe on the road. With an ancient history of being used by magicians as a psychic shield, Black Tourmaline is a vital talisman if you're a practitioner of ritual or magic. One of my Essential Rockstars, Black Tourmaline should be one of the very first crystals you add to your collection to keep you grounded as you continue down your path of sparkling, crystalline adventures.

NOTES Tourmaline is an abundant gemstone found in a range of colours. Also known as Schorl, iron-rich Black Tourmaline is the most common variety of tourmaline and by far the least expensive. Sometimes flecked with bits of silvery mica, Black Tourmaline is commonly available as both polished and raw specimens.

Turquoise

EARTH WISDOM + WHOLENESS + PROTECTION + INTEGRITY

✳ **Colour** Bright shades of blue + green

⊘ **Born in** USA, China, Tibet, Iran

☍ **Chakras** Throat, 3rd Eye

◌ **Water Cleansing** ☒ Y ☐ N

MAGIC Bright Turquoise – holy, sacred, protective, healing – has an ancient history as a revered gemstone, long beloved by indigenous cultures, royalty, and hippie glam alike. A classic adornment on boho fingers and wrists the world over, Turquoise's history as sacred jewellery stretches back through the mists of time as one of the first stones to be used for human jewellery. Native Americans revere Turquoise as a representation of *Earth Consciousness*, bridging heaven and earth: Blue Turquoise = Father Sky, Green Turquoise = Mother Earth. Wear this stone to strengthen your commitment to walking lightly on our planet, and to living in awareness and reverence of nature and its cycles. A stone of folklore wisdom and natural magic, Turquoise magnifies the connection to your own indigenous histories. Worn as a protective talisman by everyone from the Aztecs and Ancient Egyptians, to modern Tibetans and Native Americans, Turquoise forms a protective armour around you, shielding and strengthening as you walk bravely forward in Truth and Integrity.

NOTES Turquoise forms as non-crystallised masses. Imitation Turquoise is extremely common, especially blue-dyed Howlite (sometimes sold as Howlite Turquoise). A protective talisman believed to warn its wearer of danger or illness by changing colour, Turquoise's hue can indeed deepen from absorbed body oils, although 90% of modern Turquoise is impermeable as it's been 'stabilised', a chemical process that hardens specimens to make them suitable for jewellery. Turquoise is a traditional birthstone for December, and a zodiac birthstone for Sagittarius, Scorpio, and Pisces.

Yulia Van Doren

'A few years ago, after a move from bustling Manhattan to a mystical little town in California's Gold Rush foothills, my night time dreams were suddenly flooded with glittering visions of crystals, gold and gemstones. The idea for a bright and modern approach to crystals consumed my imagination, and I dove headfirst into rapidly expanding my knowledge of crystals and crystal healing, something I had explored since childhood but never with this intensity. I quickly connected with many people around the world who resonate with crystals presented in a modern, light-filled way; although we love tradition, we are also excited to be taking crystals out of the dimly-lit corners and cases where they've traditionally been kept to give them the bright, centre-stage spotlight they deserve in which to sparkle, shine and share their healing gifts.'

Yulia Van Doren is a Grammy-nominated classical singer and sound healer. Her work has received extensive international acclaim, including features by the *New York Times*, *Financial Times* and **mindbodygreen**, among many others. Passionate about holistic wellness, Yulia launched Goldirocks, a modern crystal brand, via Instagram in 2015. With a unique focus on presenting crystal healing in a modern, accessible and relatable style, Goldirocks has rapidly risen in popularity to become one of the most visible crystal brands, with a loyal following of celebrities and holistic wellness gurus. Yulia shares performances, workshops and private healing sessions worldwide, and lives in Northern California.

WWW.GOLDIROCKS.CO

@GOLDIROCKS.CO

THANK YOU:

Mother Earth for these holy healing gifts

Harriet, Vanessa, Erika and Jenny for your vision, patience and
inspiration as we created this book. It has been an honour,
I am so grateful!

Norma Gentile for immeasurable gifts of healing, support and
inspiration, as well as input on chakras

Forrest Cureton for kind help with mineral localities

Hailey for always being at the other end of Skype at every step
of this crazy project

My siblings Sophia, Natalia, Daniel, Sarah, Leya, Aaron, Eliyana, my
mother and father, my grandmothers, the Purtill family, my ancestors,
and my dear friends: I love you all more than words can say. It is such
a blessing to get to go through life with you. Thank you, thank you,
thank you.

My Justin for supporting every. single. one. of my crazy ideas with
encouraging enthusiasm and never-ending love. You are my rock,
thank you for both grounding me and letting me fly simultaneously.

And to all of my Instagram *friends* ('followers' is much too formal!):
you have been the kindest imaginable support squad for this
crystalline adventure since the very first day. **This book goes out
to all you sacred rebels, healers, and magic-makers: thank you for
making our shared world a brighter and more sparkling place.**
You rock!

CRYSTAL INDEX

FSC

www.fsc.org

MIX

Paper from
responsible sources

FSC™ C020056

Publishing Director Sarah Lavelle
Creative Director Helen Lewis
Editor Harriet Butt
Art Direction and Design Vanessa Masci
Photographer Erika Raxworthy
Prop stylist Priscilla Moscatt
Production Nikolaus Ginelli, Vincent Smith

First published in 2017 Quadrille,
an imprint of Hardie Grant Publishing

Quadrille
52–54 Southwark Street
London SE1 1UN
quadrille.com

Reprinted in 2017, 2018 (six times), 2019
(three times), 2020 (five times), 2021
20 19 18 17

Cataloguing in Publication Data: a catalogue
record for this book is available from the
British Library.

ISBN: 978 1 78713 035 7
Printed in China

*No medical claims are made for the stones in this
book and the information given is not intended
to act as a substitute for medical treatment. The
healing properties are given for guidance only
and are, for the most part, based on anecdotal
evidence and/or traditional therapeutic use.
The advice in this book is intended solely for
informational and educational purposes and
not as medical advice. If in any doubt, a crystal
healing practitioner or medical professional should
be consulted.*

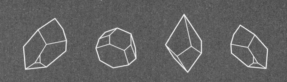